MENTAL FLOSS

THE CURIOUS VIEWER

MF ULTIMATE

TV

TRIVIA

& QUIZ

BOOK

EDITED BY
JENNIFER M. WOOD
AND THE TEAM AT
MENTAL FLOSS

weldon**owen**

CEO Raoul Goff

VP PUBLISHER Roger Shaw

EDITORIAL DIRECTOR Katie Killebrew

SENIOR EDITOR Karyn Gerhard

VP CREATIVE Chrissy Kwasnik

ART DIRECTOR Allister Fein

VP MANUFACTURING Alix Nicholaeff

PRODUCTION MANAGER Sam Taylor

weldon**owen**

an imprint of Insight Editions

P.O. Box 3088

San Rafael, CA 94912

www.weldonowen.com

Copyright © 2022 Sportority Inc.

Library of Congress Cataloging-in-
Publication data is available.

ISBN 978-1-68188-849-1

Produced by Indelible Editions

INDELIBLE
EDITIONS

Printed in Turkey

2025 2024 2023 2022 • 10 9 8 7 6 5 4 3 2 1

PICTURE CREDITS

CONTENTS

INTRODUCTION

One of the many things that has always united Mental Floss's creative team with our readers is our boundless curiosity about the world around us, including our favorite TV shows. Whether it's attempting to get a firm answer on what happened at the end of *The Sopranos*, discovering the origins of Jason Sudeikis's *Ted Lasso* character, learning why Donald Glover describes *Atlanta* as "*Curb Your Enthusiasm* for rappers," or asking an ornithologist if it would be possible for Daenerys Targaryen's dragons to fly in real life as they do on *Game of Thrones*, there's no television topic too niche for our team to explore, nor is there any question too ridiculous for us to ask and get answered. There's no arguing that we're in a Golden Age of streaming, where quality content is being produced at breakneck speed—some of it good, some of it not so good, some of it great, but much of it bingeable.

So just how much do you remember about the greatest TV shows and most famous stars of the past twenty years? Contained within these pages, you'll find fascinating details about some of the best series to grace the small screen, plus space to jot down your own thoughts on topics ranging from the TV antiheroes you love to hate to the shows that had you laughing, crying— or both—for days on end. In addition, there are quizzes to test how much of a television buff you really are.

Think you've got what it takes to be considered a true Television Trivia Master (™ pending)? Read on to see if you can reign supreme.

FANTASTIC TELEVISION PILOTS

1 *Lost* // **"Pilot, Parts I and 2"**
It's been more than a decade since *Lost* went off the air with a series finale that still prompts debate from fans. But if we must continue to argue that the show didn't satisfyingly conclude its mystery-laden run for some, at least we can all agree that it started with a bang. The two-part pilot of *Lost*, which established the show's trademark use of flashbacks to explore its characters, is a thrilling piece of controlled chaos, introducing mystery after mystery (that polar bear!) and revealing almost immediately that a phenomenon was lying in wait to ensnare us.

2 *The West Wing* // **"Pilot"**
In some ways, the first episode of *The West Wing* is all a witty, engaging buildup to one legendary moment: when President Josiah Bartlet (Martin Sheen) finally emerges after riding his bicycle into a tree, just so he can smack down some powerful Christian leaders who've been troubling his staff all day. In other ways, even without the president's appearance to cap it off, *The West Wing*'s pilot is a near-flawless chronicle of the power behind the throne and of brilliant people just trying to do their best in an imperfect system. Either way, it's an unforgettable start.

First impressions are crucial in television, where viewers need to quickly decide whether a show's characters and premise are worth watching. These pilots stuck the landing.

3 *Deadwood* // "Deadwood"

The Western was once an essential piece of scripted television programming, but when creator David Milch decided to bring his own version of Western storytelling to HBO with *Deadwood*, what we got was far removed from *Gunsmoke*. To understand that *Deadwood* was different, all you had to do was hear any character at all speak—and not just because they were cursing up a storm. There was a musicality and depth to Milch's scripting that became the show's trademark and part of its legacy.

4 *Arrested Development* // "Pilot"

Many sitcoms need at least one season to fully take shape and figure out what they're going to be, as many fans of *Parks and Recreation* and the American adaptation of *The Office* might attest. The concept is there, but the complete picture is not. *Arrested Development* is not one of those shows. Within just a few chaotic minutes onboard a yacht in the middle of an SEC raid, creator Mitch Hurwitz revealed to us one of the most hilariously dysfunctional TV families ever, and the series never looked back.

5 *Freaks and Geeks* // "Pilot"

Few television series, let alone sitcoms, have ever managed to pull off as delicate a tonal balance in quite the same way that *Freaks and Geeks* did, even in its very first episode. The pilot is a meditation on fitting in, bullying, parental pressure, young love, what it means to be "cool," and the often-vast disparities between different kinds of teenagers—and it manages to get each of those things right all at once. "Pilot" is the announcement of one of the greatest cult shows ever made, and though the show is distinctly set in the 1980s, its stories feel timeless.

BLUTH COMPANY

Once Upon a Crime

Does crime *really* pay? The smartest way to answer that question is vicariously, and via fictional characters. These are some of our favorites.

Deadwood (2004–2006)

Like many of the prestige dramas that HBO aired in the wake of the success of *The Sopranos*, David Milch's *Deadwood* managed to attract a small but rabid fan base that has only grown with time. Set in the late 1800s, not long after Custer's Last Stand, the show mixes fact with fiction as historical characters—including Wild Bill Hickok (Keith Carradine), Calamity Jane (Robin Weigert), and Wyatt Earp (Gale Harold)—make their way in and out of Deadwood, South Dakota. Its main characters—Seth Bullock (Timothy Olyphant), Sol Star (John Hawkes), and Al Swearengen (Ian McShane)—were also real people.

While *Deadwood* includes all of the tropes we've come to expect of a great Western, including gunfights, gold rushes, and fun-filled brothels, the series is really about the evolution of civilization and how we build communities out of chaos—with a lot of f-bombs dropped along the way, mostly by McShane.

Milch was dedicated to getting the tone of the Black Hills right. It was a dangerous and gruff place where men toiled, fought, and cursed. But the curse words of the 1870s would seem downright laughable today. So *tarnation* and *goldarn* were swapped for contemporary cursing's heavy hitters, even though *fuck* didn't come into popularity until the 1920s. According to one dedicated viewer, the entire series clocked in with 2,980 f-bombs. While that beats out the 506 times the expletive was used in 2013's

MATCH THE CRIMINAL TO THEIR TV SERIES:

____ 1. Nucky Thompson A. *Peaky Blinders*

____ 2. Boyd Crowder B. *The Wire*

____ 3. Polly Gray C. *Fargo*

____ 4. Ralph Cifaretto D. *Justified*

____ 5. Omar Little E. *Boardwalk Empire*

____ 6. Floyd Gerhardt F. *The Sopranos*

The Wolf of Wall Street, Martin Scorsese's curse-laden white-collar crime drama wins when you break it down by uses per minute, boasting 2.81 f-bombs per minute to *Deadwood's* 1.56.

Peaky Blinders (2013–present)

This gritty period piece, created by Steven Knight, is essentially the British *Godfather* and was inspired by the real-life gang that operated in Birmingham, England, during the nineteenth and twentieth centuries. (They reportedly got their name from the razor blades they sewed into the brims of their caps, though some historians question whether they actually did that.)

Cillian Murphy stars as Tommy Shelby, the sprawling gang's reluctant but fiery leader who must take over the family business out of a sense of criminal duty. Scored with a modern soundtrack (it's the best use of Nick Cave & the Bad Seeds "Red Right Hand" ever) and shot with a

classically staged intensity, *Peaky Blinders* gets its bingeability from constantly confronting the viewer with how people doing such wrong could seem so right.

The series has also featured a number of acclaimed guest stars, including Oscar winner Adrien Brody as Luca Changretta, an Italian American who comes to England to avenge his father (who was murdered by the Peaky Blinders). Meanwhile, Oscar nominee Tom Hardy plays marble-mouthed Jewish gangster Alfie Solomons, the ruthless leader of a rival gang, in what is among the more intense roles of the infamously intense actor's repertoire. Each season is just six episodes—easy enough to devour over a weekend.

Warrior (2019–present)

Warrior, the brainchild of *Banshee* creator Jonathan Tropper, is based on an original idea by Bruce Lee about a martial arts prodigy who emigrates from China in search of his sister. Andrew Koji plays Ah Sahm, the young expert who travels to San Francisco only to encounter crime, corruption, and a bustling Asian community in turmoil.

In 1972, Lee's original concept was retooled and subsequently retitled *Kung Fu*, starring David Carradine, which meant that *Warrior*'s executive producer Shannon Lee (Bruce's daughter) and film director Justin Lin (*The Fast and the Furious* film series) felt an even greater obligation to get the story right. The two have shepherded *Warrior* to great reviews for its ability to showcase both blinding action and the beauty of the culture from which the iconic martial artist came. And they did it just in time: *Warrior* was the final series green-lit by Cinemax before the network ceased production of original programming, hence the series' jump to HBO Max.

Interestingly, almost none of the main cast members are actually from the country of their respective characters, so in addition to English, Japanese actor Koji having to learn Chinese phonetically to play Ah Sahm, almost all of his co-stars (including those in white roles) had to learn different accents to play their parts as authentically as possible.

Which story from history would you like to see adapted into a TV show?

WHY:

JUST SAY YES

From marijuana to meth, drugs are really just a sidebar to these deeply layered stories about family, friendship, and power dynamics.

The Wire (2002–2008)

In "The Wire," the sixth episode of *The Wire*'s first season, Detective Lester Freamon (Clarke Peters) tells perpetual screwup Roland "Prez" Pryzbylewski (Jim True-Frost), "All the pieces matter." Freamon says this while teaching the junior detective the basics of good police work and why it's essential to consider each bit of evidence both on its own and as part of the overall puzzle. While it could have easily been written off as a throwaway line, the idea that "all the pieces matter" came to embody the overall theme of *The Wire* itself, which is one of the most deeply layered shows ever to grace the small screen.

Though it never garnered many awards or even boasted solid viewership numbers during its time on the air, *The Wire* has regularly been cited as one of the greatest television shows of all time—right alongside *The Sopranos, Mad Men,* and *Breaking Bad*—by the likes of outlets such as *Entertainment Weekly, Rolling Stone*, and *Empire*. On paper, it might sound like just another cops-versus-

Which future Oscar nominee was *The Wire* creator David Simon's first choice to play the role of Detective Jimmy McNulty?

A. Willem Dafoe
B. Idris Elba
C. Clive Owen
D. Ethan Hawke
E. John C. Reilly
F. Philip Seymour Hoffman

criminals series, but the truth (like the show itself) is far more complex. Over the course of its five seasons, the carefully plotted drama upends every cops-and-robbers trope ever seen on television. In doing so, it weaves an intricate portrait of the inner workings of the city of Baltimore and the roles that not only the police and criminal elements play in the shaping of Charm City, but the roles played by the city's politicians, educators, and the media, too.

The Wire has been compared to the works of William Shakespeare and Charles Dickens, but as creator David Simon told Slate, "In our heads, we're writing a Greek tragedy. But instead of the gods being petulant and jealous Olympians hurling lightning bolts down at our protagonists, it's the postmodern institutions that are the gods. And they are gods. And no one is bigger."

Weeds (2005–2012)

In 2005, Showtime took a risk when they bought writer Jenji Kohan's concept for Weeds, a comedy-drama that goes to some pretty dark places over its eight impressive seasons. Nancy Botwin (Mary-Louise Parker) is a basic, Starbucks-sipping suburban mom who has turned to selling pot to maintain her family's upper-middle-class lifestyle following the sudden death of her husband Judah (Jeffrey Dean Morgan). Nancy is torn between crafting a stable life of comfort for her two children, Silas (Hunter Parrish) and Shane (Alexander Gould), and the siren song of large piles of cash that comes from digging deeper into the criminal underworld.

For eight seasons and 102 episodes, viewers followed the exploits of the Botwins, from Nancy being a suburban dealer to her marrying the drug lord and mayor of Tijuana Esteban Reyes (Oscar nominee Demián Bichir). Of course, a lot of weed was smoked on the show, which

Bichir revealed to GQ was actually lettuce. Marijuana may be central to the show, but according to Kohan, the title (and the overall vibe) also refers to "hardy plants struggling to survive"—a perfect distillation of its characters.

Breaking Bad (2008–2013)

As Breaking Bad was coming to a close in 2013, Bryan Cranston received an email from a fan congratulating him for his work on the series. "Your performance as Walter White was the best acting I have seen—ever," it read, with compliments extended to the entire cast. The letter was sent by Sir Anthony Hopkins.

During its five seasons, Breaking Bad elicited that kind of enthusiasm from millions of viewers—for its actors, for its sweeping portrayal of a sweltering New Mexico drug scene, and for its anxiety-provoking story about a high school chemistry teacher (Cranston) who is diagnosed with lung cancer and decides it would be better to use what time he has left to make some quick cash by cooking methamphetamine than to leave his family financially compromised.

As Walt descends further into the abyss, shaping his morality to fit the circumstances, the audience is tugged along with him, torn between the inherent ugliness of his criminality and his relatable devotion to his family. Creator Vince Gilligan described it as affable teacher Mr. Chips becoming Scarface. For the audience, it was another kind of transformation: a television show with the urgency of a page-turning thriller that left them exhilarated and exhausted. Years after its finale, getting into a casual chat about favorite shows on TV will inevitably lead to someone asking, "You've watched Breaking Bad, right?" The answer is usually yes. A better question might be: How many times?

SHOWS I STARTED BUT NEVER FINISHED

1 _____
WHY: _____

2 _____
WHY: _____

3 _____
WHY: _____

4 _____
WHY: _____

5 _____
WHY: _____

SUPREME JUSTICE

Watching these lawyers skewer an adversary in the boardroom or the courtroom will have you wondering if maybe you should've gone to law school after all.

The Good Wife
(2009–2016)

Many critics consider *The Good Wife*—created by Michelle and Robert King (*Evil*)—to be network television's last great drama before the arrival of the streaming era. The series revolves around Alicia Florrick (Julianna Margulies), the wife of Illinois State's Attorney Peter Florrick (Chris Noth), who returns to work as a litigator in the wake of her husband's political corruption and sex scandals. Inspired by the real-life improprieties of President Bill Clinton and North Carolina Senator John Edwards, the Kings created a complex character exploring her own agency as she emerges from the shadow of her husband's ambitions.

Despite the show's success and longevity, there were unconfirmed rumors of a feud between Margulies and her co-star Archie Panjabi, whose characters play best friends but do not share any screen time for the final fifty episodes—which is particularly noticeable in a final scene, where it's clear they shot their lines separately with green screens and body doubles. Though *The Good Wife* aired its final episode in 2016, it branched off into *The Good Fight*, a spin-off starring Christine Baranski, in 2017.

MATCH THE LAWYER TO THE TV SERIES:

_____ I. Howard Hamlin

_____ 2. Diane Lockhart

_____ 3. Jack McCoy

_____ 4. Patty Hewes

_____ 5. Alan Shore

_____ 6. Wayne Jarvis

A. *Law & Order*

B. *Boston Legal*

C. *Better Call Saul*

D. *Arrested Development*

E. *The Good Wife*

F. *Damages*

Suits (2011–2019)

On June 23, 2011, USA Network debuted a law drama called *Suits*, created by former sitcom writer Aaron Korsh. The show is about a college dropout named Mike Ross (Patrick J. Adams) who passes the bar exam but doesn't have a law degree. Ross stumbles into an interview with Pearson Specter Litt partner Harvey Specter (Gabriel Macht), who quickly learns Ross's secret. Despite Ross's lack of a law degree, Specter decides to hire him as an associate based on Ross's ability to memorize law facts and Specter's own desire to give Ross a second chance at life.

Before becoming a TV writer and showrunner, Korsh worked on Wall Street as an investment banker, which was the original profession for the *Suits* characters. "I worked for a guy named Harvey, I had a good memory, and I had a dalliance with marijuana," Korsh told Collider. He quit Wall Street in the early 1990s, moved to Los Angeles, and became a writer's assistant. "I wrote a spec piece that I originally intended to be a half-hour *Entourage*-type [show] based on my experiences working on Wall Street, but as I wrote it, I started realizing it wants to be an hour-long show," he told *The Hollywood Reporter.*

As a first-time showrunner, Korsh felt inexperienced, which only helped develop the show's characters: "I think it was the first day on set, shooting the pilot, and inside I was like, 'What am I doing here?

REPLAY

Before Bob Odenkirk was an Emmy-nominated actor in *Better Call Saul*, he was an Emmy-winning comedy writer who worked on *The Ben Stiller Show, Late Night with Conan O'Brien, The Dennis Miller Show, The Dana Carvey Show, Tenacious D,* and *Saturday Night Live,* where he created the character of Matt Foley (Chris Farley), the motivational speaker who "lives in a van down by the *river.*"

people, including fellow lawyer and perfectly ponytailed Kim Wexler (Rhea Seehorn)—he cares about winning more, despite his better instincts. Played with exhausting enthusiasm by Odenkirk, Jimmy's journey to strip-mall success is as harrowing and taut as watching Walter White navigate the meth business, but it's (thankfully) another animal altogether.

While whittling down a huge pile of ideas into what would become *Breaking Bad*'s scripts, Vince Gilligan and the other writers had a lot of lines for Saul that got scrapped. "We love writing for the character," Gilligan told Uproxx in 2015. "We love putting words in his mouth. And we had so much fun, indeed, doing that, that it started as a lark; we'd come up with some great term or phrase, and we'd laugh about it in the writers' room. And then we'd say, 'You know, when we're doing the Saul Goodman show we'll be able to blah, blah, blah.'" Be careful what you joke about.

I'm a fraud,' which is the basis of Mike being a fraud."

Better Call Saul (2015–2022)

Before he was Saul Goodman, lawyer to everyone's favorite chemistry-teacher-turned-meth-kingpin Walter White on *Breaking Bad,* Bob Odenkirk was Jimmy McGill, the ne'er-do-well brother to highly respected Albuquerque attorney Chuck McGill (Michael McKean). Though deep down, Jimmy clearly cares about people—well, some

What's your favorite TV spin-off? _____

WHY: _____

Uncivil Service

Whether in real life or on the small screen, there's really no such thing as "politics as usual," as these shows attest.

The West Wing (1999–2006)

Aaron Sorkin's benchmark political drama was prestige TV before we even started using the term. *The West Wing* focuses on the presidential administration of the fictional Democrat Josiah "Jed" Bartlet (Martin Sheen) and his trusty team of political wunderkinds, including best friend and chief of staff Leo McGarry (John Spencer), deputy chief of staff Josh Lyman (Bradley Whitford), communications director Toby Ziegler (Richard Schiff), deputy communications director Sam Seaborn (Rob Lowe), press secretary C. J. Cregg (Allison Janney), and personal aide Charlie Young (Dulé Hill).

The West Wing rose above early doubts to become one of the most celebrated shows of its era, winning four consecutive Outstanding Drama Series Emmys and turning its ensemble cast into major stars. With its lightning-quick dialogue (a Sorkin signature), eye for authenticity, and plenty of walk-and-talks (another Sorkin trademark), the series is as close as most will likely ever get to seeing how the White House operates during moments of mundanity and complete chaos.

Sheen accepted the role of President Bartlet thinking he would be appearing in just a handful of episodes each season. Sorkin originally intended to use the president sparingly out of fear that having the leader of the free world pop up all the time would "take up all the oxygen in a room." But when Sheen showed up to work on the show, in the famous final scene of the pilot in which he berates a group of hypocritical ministers, everyone knew Bartlet needed to have a larger presence.

24 (2001–2010)

With its American tough-guy hero and a conveyor belt of terrorist attacks to foil, *24* accidentally became the zeitgeist marker for 2000s television. The series, which started filming before 9/11 but premiered just two months after the terrorist attacks, stars Kiefer Sutherland as Counter Terrorist Unit (CTU) officer Jack Bauer and tells an epic story of imminent threats and last-minute saves to the soundtrack of a beeping clock. It was an innovative show that presented events in as close to real-time as anything with commercials could get, filling an hour slot with an hour of in-universe action. The structure of this espionage thriller was perfect

MATCH THE FICTIONAL PRESIDENT TO THE TV SERIES:

_____ 1. Richard Splett   A. *The West Wing*

_____ 2. Claire Underwood   B. *Scandal*

_____ 3. Mackenzie Allen   C. *1600 Penn*

_____ 4. Fitzgerald Grant   D. *Designated Survivor*

_____ 5. Matthew Santos   E. *Supergirl*

_____ 6. Allison Taylor   F. *Veep*

_____ 7. Tom Kirkland   G. *The Leftovers*

_____ 8. The Most Powerful   H. *Commander in Chief*
Man in the World
    I. *24*

_____ 9. Dale Gilchrist

_____ 10. Olivia Marsden   J. *House of Cards*

for making the audience feel the claustro-phobic constraints of having to work faster than your enemies.

Nuclear weapon detonations, cyber-attacks, and beyond—Bauer hustled to prevent them all from happening, regardless of the required methods. The end (almost) always justified the means in Bauer's mind, which is why the show took on both the good and the evil elements of the post-9/11 culture in America.

Presidents didn't make out so well on *24*: The show went through a series of presidents in eighteen years (of in-universe time, as each season was generally set at least eighteen months after the previous chapter), getting rid of its POTUSes using everything from assassinations to potential Alzheimer's disease. Of those, President David Palmer (Dennis Haysbert) was the only one elected to office who actually finished a full term.

The Thick of It (2005–2012)

Armando Iannucci's BAFTA-winning British government satire featured future *Doctor Who* star Peter Capaldi as the delightfully sadistic Malcolm Tucker, the Prime Minister's chief enforcer, who spends his days chewing up—and chewing out—a rotating cast of cabinet ministers. This is the show that eventually birthed *Veep*, as well as the 2009 film *In the Loop* (both Iannucci creations), and features a lot of the same tonal conventions of egomaniacs failing upward, petty tyrants concerned with office politics, and the crushing absurdity of trying (or not trying) to govern.

The show is infamous for its inventive swearing, going so far as to hire writer Ian Martin as the show's official "swearing consultant." Martin's work can be heard in the very first episode, when Tucker is on the phone and remarks, "He's as fucking useless as a marzipan dildo" (the original line had simply been: "He's fucking useless"). Martin eventually became a full-fledged member of the show's writing staff and went on to write for *Veep* as well. (*Succession* creator Jesse Armstrong was also a writer on the series.)

Veep (2012–2019)

Seven years after creating *The Thick of It*, Armando Iannucci took his satirical sensibilities to Washington, DC. *Veep* stars Julia Louis-Dreyfus as the charismatic, but mostly ineffectual, Vice President Selina Meyer. The show brutally skewers government bureaucracy and ambition, as Selina's staff members compete to gain favor with their superiors. Unlike the utopian presidency of *The West Wing*, the characters in *Veep* are driven completely by self-interest and are more focused on the appearance of success than actually making things happen. Louis-Dreyfus won six consecutive Outstanding Lead Actress in a Comedy Series Emmy Awards for *Veep*, the most ever for an actor for the same role.

Veep pokes, prods, and derides the DC bubble while diving into the complexities of the political arena. It's a refreshing take on a political series—one that knows it's dealing with heavy subjects but refuses to take itself too seriously. However, *Veep* obviously struck a chord in DC: Associate Justice of the Supreme Court Elena Kagan once told Louis-Dreyfus that she would have lunch once a week with the late justice Antonin Scalia, where they would talk about *Veep*.

Which fictional TV politician would you most like to see in office?

WHY: _____

BLUES & TWOS

Bobbies. Bizzies. Rozzers. Beyond a range of new slang terms, British crime shows often have a bit more grit and circumstance over their American counterparts.

Sherlock (2010-2017)

Although Sherlock Holmes ranks as one of the most frequently adapted fictional characters of all time, the producers of BBC's Emmy-nominated *Sherlock* have managed to make the detective seem as fresh as when his print adventures first began appearing in 1887.

For years, writers Steven Moffat and Mark Gatiss took a train to and from Cardiff while working on *Doctor Who* and discussed various projects they were interested in working on; one that repeatedly came up was a modern-day adaptation of Sir Arthur Conan Doyle's legendary sleuth, Sherlock Holmes. This went on for some time, with neither man making any particular effort to get it off the ground, until Moffat's wife, producer Sue Vertue, decided to invite them both to lunch at the Criterion, an iconic watering hole and eatery in London's Piccadilly Circus. It's the same place where the fictional John Watson, Sherlock's best friend, first hears of the famed detective. The two got the hint and began working on the series.

Though playing the eponymous "consulting detective" in *Sherlock* is the role that brought Benedict Cumberbatch global recognition, saying yes to the part wasn't exactly a no-brainer for the actor. While speaking at a BAFTA event in 2014, Cumberbatch admitted that he was a little hesitant to sign on for the project, as he was worried "It could be a bit cheap and cheesy." Then he learned who was at the helm of the project.

"My mum had done a few episodes of *Coupling* with Steven [Moffat] and Mark Gatiss was a huge hero of mine when I was a student in *League of Gentleman*," Cumberbatch said, "so I knew the stable was good. I thought I would read it and then I fell in love with it."

Recommended Binge-Watching: British Crime Dramas

Bodyguard (2018–present)
Endeavour (2012–present)
The Fall (2013–2016)
Grantchester (2014–present)
Happy Valley (2014–2016, 2022)
Informer (2018)
Line of Duty (2012–2021)
Marcella (2016–2021)
Midsomer Murders (1997–present)
Miss Fisher's Murder Mysteries (2012–2015)
Unforgotten (2015–present)
Vera (2011–present)

Luther (2010-2019)

For just about as long as there have been police dramas, there have been conflicted cops at the center of those series, and *Luther* is no different. What makes the series stand out, however, is Idris Elba as DCI John Luther, a brilliant but headstrong detective who regularly finds himself on the wrong side of London's most unhinged criminals. But Luther will stop at nothing to make sure he gets the bad guy—even if he has to bend the law or enlist the help of socio-pathic genius Alice Morgan (Ruth Wilson) to do it. Even the most diabolical criminal is no match for the hulking intensity of Elba, who won a Golden Globe for the role.

Broadchurch (2013-2017)

Though it was a bona fide television phenomenon when it premiered in its native England in 2013, it took a while for American audiences to catch on to *Broadchurch*—and it's a good thing they finally did. Like a less strange version of *Twin Peaks*, the series follows two newly partnered detectives (former *Doctor Who* star David Tennant and future

 **REPLAY**

To keep people guessing who the murderer was in *Broadchurch*, creator Chris Chibnall kept everyone—including the cast—in the dark until the last minute. "For 85 percent of filming, no one had any idea who was guilty," he said. "The cast and crew set up a rogues' gallery and took bets on who they thought it was, but I was determined that secrecy was the key to the drama's success."

Oscar winner Olivia Colman) tasked with solving the murder of a twelve-year-old boy in a tiny seaside town where everyone knows each other, and everyone is a suspect.

In addition to being a phenomenal crime procedural that keeps you guessing until the very end, *Broadchurch* is not afraid to take its viewers into the darkest corners of the human psyche, yet it still maintains a message that reminds us we have the power to bounce back from even the worst tragedies.

Poirot (1989-2013)

"David Suchet is the definitive Hercule Poirot," Eirik Dragsund, Agatha Christie expert, told *The New York Times*, referring to the leading actor of *Poirot*, based on the long-running series of Agatha Christie mysteries about the fussy Belgian with a pristine mustache and superior "little grey cells." The show follows the classic mystery formula: introducing a cast of characters and suspects, drawing the invincible private detective's attention, and then barreling toward a logical-yet-surprising conclusion.

These loving adaptations of the legendary mystery writer's stories add serious production value and human depth to the proceedings, bringing early 1900s England to full Art Deco form as *Poirot* brings the killer(s) to justice. In addition to Suchet, Hugh Fraser (Captain Arthur Hastings), and Philip Jackson (Chief Inspector James Japp), the many soon-to-be stars that show up on the program make bingeing *Poirot* a delight. Keep an eye out for appearances from Michael Fassbender, Aidan Gillen, and Emily Blunt, among others.

Which TV detective would you most want to solve a case with? _____

WHY: _____

MATCH the quote to the *Sherlock* character who said it:

A. Sherlock Holmes

B. James Moriarty

C. Mary Watson

D. Molly Hooper

E. Dr. John Watson

F. Irene Adler (a.k.a. The Woman)

G. Mrs. Hudson

H. Mycroft Holmes

___ 1. **"I don't shave for Sherlock Holmes."**

___ 2. **"I'm not dead, let's have dinner."**

___ 3. **"All lives end. All hearts are broken."**

___ 4. **"A nice murder. That'll cheer you up."**

___ 5. **"Heroes don't exist, and if they did, I wouldn't be one of them."**

___ 6. **"Every fairy tale needs a good old-fashioned villain."**

___ 7. **"You're a bit like my dad. He's dead."**

___ 8. **"I agree. I'm the best thing that could have happened to you."**

Two Degrees of...
Idris Elba

Fill in the title of the TV show or movie that connects these actors to *Luther* star **Idris Elba**.

JENNIFER ANISTON
was in

_____
TV SHOW OR MOVIE NAME
(2005) with Mark Ruffalo, who was in

_____
TV SHOW OR MOVIE NAME
(2018) with Idris Elba.

BRYAN CRANSTON
was in

_____
TV SHOW OR MOVIE NAME
(2010) with Helen Mirren, who was in

_____
TV SHOW OR MOVIE NAME
(2019) with Idris Elba.

AMERICA FERRERA
was in

_____
TV SHOW OR MOVIE NAME
(2019) with Cate Blanchett, who was in

_____
TV SHOW OR MOVIE NAME
(2017) with Idris Elba.

KUMAIL NANJIANI
was in

TV SHOW OR MOVIE NAME
(2019) with Karen Gillan, who was in

TV SHOW OR MOVIE NAME
with Idris Elba.

ANGELA BASSETT
was in

TV SHOW OR MOVIE NAME
(1997) with Matthew McConaughey, who was in

TV SHOW OR MOVIE NAME
(2017) with Idris Elba.

NICK OFFERMAN
was in

TV SHOW OR MOVIE NAME
(2005) with Benicio del Toro, who was in

TV SHOW OR MOVIE NAME
(2018) with Idris Elba.

The *Law* & *Order*-Verse

May 24, 2010 marked the end of an era when the original *Law & Order* aired its final episode after twenty years on the air. While it has spawned a whole franchise of spin-offs, the original series is now ready for a comeback.

Law & Order (1990–2010)

At more than thirty years old, the *Law & Order* universe seems to have always been with us. Revolutionary when the mothership show (aka "original recipe") premiered in 1990, *Law & Order* began in an era when the web browser had just been invented and only five million Americans had a cell phone subscription.

The show's first episode was originally shot in 1988, with CBS as the intended airing network. That pilot, written by Dick Wolf and titled "Everybody's

Favorite Bagman," was meant to look documentary-style gritty, so it was shot on sixteen-millimeter film. But in the end, CBS passed on the pilot, and NBC president Brandon Tartikoff smartly agreed to pick up thirteen episodes of *Law & Order* for their fall 1990 schedule—two years after the pilot was shot.

Though the actors who were ultimately cast in the key original roles will forever live in our memories as the only true possibilities, it turns out that future *ER* star Eriq La Salle was originally up for the role of ADA Paul Robinette (which went to Richard Brooks), and future *Reservoir Dogs* star Michael Madsen was being seriously considered for the role of Detective Mike Logan (Chris Noth's character).

Some of the unsung heroes of NBC's *Law & Order* success story are other networks. *Law & Order* came into being on the tail end of serial dramatic TV series like *St. Elsewhere* and *Hill Street Blues*. Those shows were critically acclaimed and beloved, but the reruns performed poorly because they relied on continuing story arcs. Wolf aimed to create a procedural show that could rerun endlessly, so he made sure that very little of the characters' personal lives made it into the scripts and very few episodes linked to one another.

Enter A&E, hungry for something to fill holes in its programming schedules. The cable network began rerunning *Law & Order* episodes multiple times a day in 1995, which boosted their ratings—plus the ratings of new episodes on NBC—and made the show ubiquitous. Since then, reruns have aired on multiple networks.

Law & Order: SVU (1999–present)

Spin-offs rarely outlive their original series, and they definitely don't eclipse them in terms of longevity. But *Law & Order: Special Victims Unit* defies expectations. The series, which kicked off just before the millennium and focused the abuse and trauma of some of society's most vulnerable individuals, found its guiding light and voice early on thanks in large part to the unwavering dedication of its lead detective, Olivia Benson (Mariska Hargitay).

Originally, the show was going to be called *Law & Order: Sex Crimes* and was inspired by the so-called "Preppy Killer" case: In 1986, nineteen-year-old Robert Chambers strangled eighteen-year-old Jennifer Levin in New York City's Central Park. Dick Wolf had written a *Law & Order* episode "ripped" from that particular headline and saw a future in these kinds of stories. But NBC thought *Sex Crimes* was a bit too raw for a title. "We're going to be covering a wide range of crimes and *Special Victims Unit* just seems more inclusive," Wolf told *The New York Post* in 1999.

While the original recipe *Law & Order* turned out its lights in 2010

THE *LAW & ORDER* UNIVERSE, EXPLORED

The *Law & Order* concept proved so popular that spin-offs were inevitable—and haven't finished yet. Here's the whole of the global *Law & Order*-verse.

Law & Order (1990–2010, 2022)
Law & Order: Special Victims Unit (1999–PRESENT)
Law & Order: Criminal Intent (2001–2011)
Law & Order: Trial by Jury (2005–2006)
Conviction (2006)
Law & Order: UK (2009–2014)
Law & Order: LA (2010–2011)
Law & Order: True Crime (2017)
Law & Order: Organized Crime (2021–PRESENT)

(though it's coming back in 2022), *SVU* continues to plow forward—and create its own spin-offs. *Law & Order: Organized Crime*, starring original *SVU* cast member Christopher Meloni, premiered in April 2021 with Detective Elliot Stabler making a return to his old stomping grounds before being sent off on his own adventures.

In the years since its debut, *SVU* has become an institution unto itself, partly because it plays by its own rules.

REPLAY

Call it *dun-dun, chung-chung,* or *thunk-thunk.* The iconic sound effect that underscores key moments in each episode of *Law & Order* was created by show composer Mike Post, who told *Entertainment Weekly* that he intended for the sound to mimic a jail cell slamming shut. It's a synthesized effect that combines about seven different sounds, including the sound of hundreds of Japanese men stamping their feet on a wooden floor. By the way: Post, who also wrote the show's theme music, gets a separate royalty credit every time the sound is used. *Dun-dun!*

Who are some now-famous actors you've spotted in an episode of *Law & Order* (any franchise)?

_____ _____
_____ _____
_____ _____
_____ _____
_____ _____
_____ _____
_____ _____
_____ _____
_____ _____
_____ _____
_____ _____
_____ _____

STAR: _____
SHOW: _____

STAR: _____
SHOW: _____

STAR: _____
SHOW: _____

STAR: _____
SHOW: _____

STAR: _____
SHOW: _____

STAR: _____
SHOW: _____

STAR: _____
SHOW: _____

STAR: _____
SHOW: _____

STAR: _____
SHOW: _____

STAR: _____
SHOW: _____

STAR: _____
SHOW: _____

STAR: _____
SHOW: _____

STAR: _____
SHOW: _____

STAR: _____
SHOW: _____

STAR: _____
SHOW: _____

STAR: _____
SHOW: _____

STAR: _____
SHOW: _____

STAR: _____
SHOW: _____

STAR: _____
SHOW: _____

STAR: _____
SHOW: _____

L♥VABLE OUTLAWS

Dancing on the edge of the law, these morally complex
characters live by their own codes of conduct.

Sons of Anarchy **(2008–2014)**
Influenced by *Hamlet, Sons of Anarchy*
revolves around a family (both related by
blood and not) of Grim Reaper patch–
wearing outlaw bikers in a club known
as SAMCRO (Sons of
Anarchy Motorcycle
Club Redwood Original),
based in the fictional town
of Charming, California.
The show debuted on
September 3, 2008, and
over the course of seven
seasons, became FX's
top-rated drama.

Katey Sagal plays the
matriarch, Gemma, whose
Harley-riding son Jax
(Charlie Hunnam) is the
"Hamlet" character; he's
caught between pleasing
his mother and his step-
father, Clay (Ron Perlman),
and honoring his dead
father, John, a founding
member of SAMCRO.

Sons of Anarchy courted
controversy with its grisly
scenes of violence, show-
ing everything from a
tattoo being burned
off to a character
getting forked to
death. But as cre-
ator Kurt Sutter
explained to *The
Hollywood Reporter*,

◀ REPLAY

Stephen King was an
unabashed fan of *Sons
of Anarchy*—so much so
that creator Kurt Sutter
contacted the author
about appearing in an
episode. "He assured me
that he'd write me a
suitably nasty part," King
said, and that "he said
he'd put me on a bitchin'
Harley. How could I say
no?" In the season three
episode "Caregiver," King
played a cleaner named
Bachman—a reference to
Richard Bachman, a pen
name King has used in
the past.

"For me, all that violence—because it's
not who I am and it's not where I come
from—it's all fantasy. I might as well be
writing about wizards and fairies."

John Landgraf, CEO of FX, took
issue with some of Sutter's
ideas, including the
castration of a clown:
Sutter wanted the visual
of the detached bit hitting
the ground, FX did not.
"I totally acknowledge
the need for violence,"
Landgraf said. "It's a
violent world and a violent
show. He's portraying really
tragic, dark consequences
of violence. Kurt wants to
show it in very graphic
detail, and I want to leave
more to the imagination."

Sutter told *GQ* that all
of the violence had to be
organic, not gratuitous.
"When we're fucking
burning a tattoo with a
blowtorch off a guy's back,
that is one of the most
extreme decisions these
guys may be making, but
it's real to the world," he
said. "I love being able to
do things like that, and
playing in worlds
that allow me to
do that."

Justified (2010-2015)

Justified is based on Elmore Leonard's short story "Fire in the Hole," as well as the late author's other stories about Deputy US Marshal Raylan Givens (Timothy Olyphant).

One of *Justified*'s hallmarks is its ability to perfectly replicate Leonard's whip-smart dialogue, and much of this comes from the first assignment series creator Graham Yost gave after assembling his team of writers: Read! Each of the writers read a few of Leonard's books in order to get a better sense of the rhythms of his dialogue and the style of his storytelling. "One of the great things that I got to do in writing the pilot was actually retype a lot of Elmore's style and put it in the script," Yost told IESB. "Just the act of retyping it let me get into the language a little bit more."

To ensure that the show's writers always had Leonard's singular style of prose and dialogue at the forefront of their minds, Yost gifted them all with blue wristbands that read "WWED" for "What Would Elmore Do?"

Leonard passed away in 2013, so he fortunately did have the chance to see *Justified* bring Givens to life, and Leonard loved every second of it. He was particularly impressed with the way that Olyphant interpreted the character of Raylan. "Tim Olyphant plays the character exactly the way I wrote him. I couldn't believe it," Leonard told *The Wall Street Journal* in 2012. "There are very few actors that recite the lines exactly the way you hear them when you're writing the book."

MATCH THE ELMORE LEONARD CHARACTER TO THE ACTOR WHO PLAYED THEM ON TV:

___ I. Karen Sisco	A. Peter Falk
___ 2. Marshall Sisco	B. Luis Guzmán
___ 3. Joyce Patton	C. Carla Gugino
___ 4. Judge Bob Gibbs	D. Robert Forster
___ 5. Harry Arno	E. Beau Bridges
___ 6. Buck Torres	F. Glenne Headly

Banshee (2013-2016)

Created by Jonathan Tropper (*Warrior*) and David Schickler, *Banshee* follows a mysterious ex-convict played by Antony Starr (*The Boys*) who assumes the identity of Lucas Hood, a murdered sheriff in Pennsylvania Amish Country, in order to hide from the crime lord (Ben Cross) on his tail. Throughout the show's four seasons, Hood (we never do learn the character's real name) struggles to maintain his secret identity as a lawman while continuing to embrace criminal enterprises, eventually running afoul of a local kingpin named Kai Proctor (Ulrich Thomsen).

The series marked Cinemax's first stab at original programming to compete with its sister channel HBO. Despite being set in Pennsylvania, the show wasn't actually filmed there until its fourth season, when North Carolina's elimination of production incentives drove it to the Northeast for greater authenticity (and some sweet tax credits).

DOING TIME

Life behind bars probably isn't anything like what you expected—at least not if you're watching these acclaimed series.

Oz (1997–2003)

In the late 1990s, HBO was looking to expand its original programming to include hour-long dramas. The network was intrigued by writer and producer Tom Fontana's pitch about a maximum security prison and a specific area, dubbed Emerald City, where prisoners could have more leeway in the hopes it would allow for their rehabilitation. *Oz*, which premiered on July 12, 1997, laid the groundwork for the dozens of risk-

taking, novel, and novelistic HBO shows to follow.

Oz's viewers were in for a shock: The show featured the kind of graphic violence and casual nudity you'd find in an actual prison. But viewers were also sometimes puzzled by Fontana's narrative habit of putting prisoner Augustus Hill (Harold Perrineau) in front of the camera for fourth-wall-breaking soliloquies. Fontana said he chose this approach because "in prison, guys aren't that forthcoming about what they think and what they feel 'cause that leaves them open and vulnerable to attack [. . .] So my thought was to just let someone articulate some thoughts about what all this craziness meant."

Prison Break (2005–2009, 2017)

Brotherly love is one thing, but purposely getting yourself arrested so that you can spring your sibling out of prison is another. That's the master plan behind *Prison Break*: a frenetic, twisty series that piles on the problems for Michael Scofield (Wentworth Miller), a structural engineer who had worked for an architecture firm that had access to the blueprints for Fox River

REPLAY

HBO's *Oz* featured a sprawling ensemble cast, which included future Oscar winner J.K. Simmons as the repugnant Vern Schillinger, head of the prison's Aryan population. In 1999, Simmons told *The New York Times* that Schillinger is "one of the few characters I've ever played that I refer to in the third person" and that he became depressed as a result of the role.

State Penitentiary, which is housing his wrongfully convicted brother Lincoln Burrows (Dominic Purcell).

In each episode, Scofield navigates a minefield of sadistic guards, the opportunistic warden, and his requisite love affair with the prison doctor. As the seasons wear on and the scope spreads beyond the prison's walls, the show gets progressively sillier. Still, with the exception of the 2017 revival (which is best skipped altogether), you'll want to do the time.

Orange Is the New Black (2013–2019)

Back when original content was still a relatively new concept for streaming platforms, Netflix unveiled *Orange Is the New Black*. Loosely based on the memoir of ex-felon Piper Kerman, the dramedy follows Piper Chapman (Taylor Schilling) as she leaves her cushy life for prison after being convicted on drug-related charges. Though prison has been explored in media countless times, *Orange Is the New Black* was one of the first shows to spotlight female convicts exclusively. The setting also opened the door for the show's makers to tell the stories of women rarely represented on-screen.

Creator Jenji Kohan knew that Schilling's Piper would appeal to network execs, but she wanted to go much deeper than that story. "In a lot of ways, Piper was my Trojan horse," Kohan told NPR in 2018. "You're not going to go into a network and sell a show on really fascinating tales of Black women, and

MATCH THE FICTIONAL PRISON TO THE TV SHOW ON WHICH IT APPEARS:

_____ 1. Elliott Bay Penitentiary

_____ 2. Stockton State Penitentiary

_____ 3. Stormcage Containment Facility

_____ 4. Virginia Central Penitentiary

_____ 5. Slabside Maximum Security Prison

A. *Sons of Anarchy*

B. *Doctor Who*

C. *Arrow*

D. *The Killing*

E. *The Following*

Latina women, and old women, and criminals. But if you take this white girl, this sort of fish out of water, and you follow her in, you can then expand your world and tell all of those other stories." It may have started out as Piper's story, but *Orange Is the New Black* evolved into an impressive ensemble showcase over its seven seasons, making it one of Netflix's longest-running series.

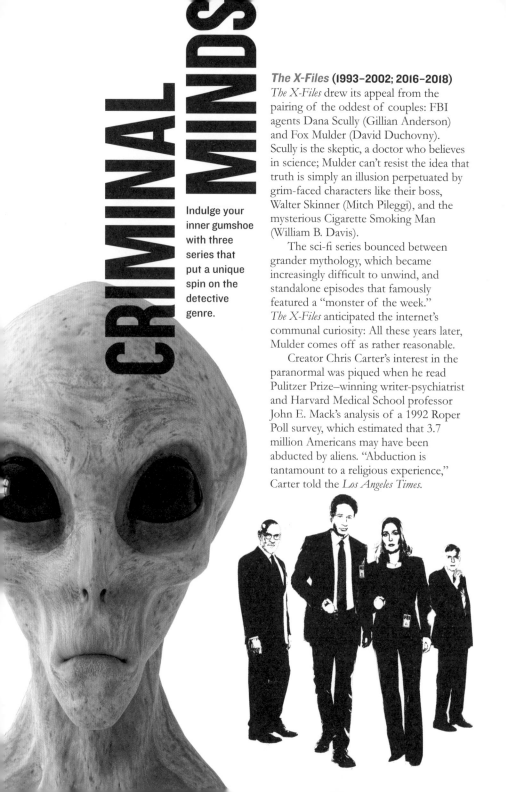

CRIMINAL MINDS

Indulge your inner gumshoe with three series that put a unique spin on the detective genre.

The X-Files (1993–2002; 2016–2018)

The X-Files drew its appeal from the pairing of the oddest of couples: FBI agents Dana Scully (Gillian Anderson) and Fox Mulder (David Duchovny). Scully is the skeptic, a doctor who believes in science; Mulder can't resist the idea that truth is simply an illusion perpetuated by grim-faced characters like their boss, Walter Skinner (Mitch Pileggi), and the mysterious Cigarette Smoking Man (William B. Davis).

The sci-fi series bounced between grander mythology, which became increasingly difficult to unwind, and standalone episodes that famously featured a "monster of the week." *The X-Files* anticipated the internet's communal curiosity: All these years later, Mulder comes off as rather reasonable.

Creator Chris Carter's interest in the paranormal was piqued when he read Pulitzer Prize–winning writer-psychiatrist and Harvard Medical School professor John E. Mack's analysis of a 1992 Roper Poll survey, which estimated that 3.7 million Americans may have been abducted by aliens. "Abduction is tantamount to a religious experience," Carter told the *Los Angeles Times*.

Carter doesn't think of the show as purely fiction. "I actually resisted the 'science fiction' label in the beginning, because the show is actually based in science," Carter told *WIRED*. "If it weren't for Scully, I think the show could be just kind of loopy. So the science and the accuracy of the science is all-important to the success of the storytelling. I think Steven Spielberg called *Close Encounters of the Third Kind* 'speculative science' and I would say *The X-Files*, for me, has always fit more into that category."

Bosch (2014–2021)

Harry Bosch (Titus Welliver), the laconic homicide detective first made famous in Michael Connelly's crime novels, scours the seedy side of Los Angeles in this winning adaptation developed by Eric Overmyer, a veteran writer and producer of such acclaimed crime series as *Homicide: Life on the Street, Law & Order*, and *The Wire*.

Don't expect any frills or explosions: *Bosch* is content to be a police procedural in the dragnet mold, and it succeeds. While *Bosch*'s seventh (and final) season premiered in the summer of 2021, that isn't the end

REPLAY

In a preview of the 1993 fall television lineup, *Entertainment Weekly* declared of *The X-Files*, "This show's a goner," citing its genre and Friday night time slot as two indicators that the series wouldn't last. Today, it's one of the longest-running sci-fi series in television history.

of the detective's story, or Welliver telling it. *Bosch: Legacy*, a spin-off featuring Welliver, Mimi Rogers, and Madison Lintz, is scheduled to premiere in 2022.

True Detective (2014–2019)

The first season of *True Detective* smashed through viewers' consciousnesses, scoring one of HBO's biggest hits, infecting pop culture with a host of bonkers quotes, and launching what is now a tripartite anthology of detective mysteries.

The vibe and look of the series' first season, which found Rust Cohle (Matthew McConaughey) and Marty Hart (Woody Harrelson) tromping through Louisiana, was crafted by director Cary Joji Fukunaga (*No Time to Die*) and marked by a jaw-dropping extended tracking shot that was unusual for TV. The next season found a trio of cops (Colin Farrell, Rachel McAdams, and Taylor Kitsch) navigating a crooked California. And in season three, Oscar winner Mahershala Ali went looking for missing girls in 1980s Arkansas. By merging hard-boiled noir and religious myth into a swirl of infectious stories, *True Detective* creator Nic Pizzolatto subverted every cop drama trope and created a genre all its own in the process.

MATCH THE DETECTIVE TO THE TV SERIES:

____ 1. Dale Cooper

____ 2. Kima Greggs

____ 3. Robert Goren

____ 4. Claudette Wyms

____ 5. Jake Peralta

A. *The Wire*

B. *The Shield*

C. *Brooklyn Nine-Nine*

D. *Twin Peaks*

E. *Law & Order: Criminal Intent*

What's one show you'd like to see make a comeback?

_____

_____

33

SHOWS THAT I LOVE THAT CRITICS HATE

SHOW: _____

WHY: _____

SHOW: _____

WHY: _____

SHOW: _____

WHY: _____

SHOW: _____

WHY: _____

SHOW: _____

WHY: _____

SHOW: _____

WHY: _____

SHOW: _____

WHY: _____

SHOW: _____

WHY: _____

SHOW: _____

WHY: _____

SHOW: _____

WHY: _____

SHOW: _____

WHY: _____

SHOW: _____

WHY: _____

SHOW: _____

WHY: _____

SHOW: _____

WHY: _____

Men Behaving Badly

How many redeeming qualities does a man need in order to be considered an antihero rather than an antagonist? These much beloved, morally questionable characters have apparently figured it out.

The Sopranos (1999-2007)

In the mafia, there's the family—the gang of career criminals, capos, bosses, and assorted misfits that drive an underground network of thuggery. And then there's family—the spouses, kids, and in-laws who can prove equally stressful. It's enough to drive a mobster to therapy, and that's where we find Tony Soprano (James Gandolfini), the simmering New Jersey crime boss, at the start of *The Sopranos*.

The demands of Tony's crime brood are often in conflict with his domestic life. His wife, Carmela (Edie Falco), tries to look the other way. His kids, Meadow (Jamie-Lynn Sigler) and A. J. (Robert Iler), are no better off as a result of their father's murky profession. Tony breaks omertà, the mafia's code of silence, only with therapist Dr. Jennifer Melfi (Lorraine Bracco), but he might as well be talking directly to the audience, who has spent decades witnessing mafia antics in *The Godfather* and *Goodfellas*

while only rarely pausing to explore its psychological effects. *The Sopranos*—which was originally developed as a movie pitch—drew its power and accolades from examining the collateral damage of violence. Like Tony, the show could explode at a moment's notice, and it could also be introspective and quiet, lapsing into whispered dinner conversations and dream sequences. Is it the best television series ever made? With decades of "peak TV" in the can, that becomes more and more subjective. Was it television at its best? Fuhgeddaboudit.

The Shield (2002-2008)

When it comes to anti-heroes, few have been quite as arresting as Vic Mackey (Michael Chiklis), the "different kind of cop" who murders, plunders, and lies his way through the politics of Los Angeles law enforcement in *The Shield*.

Chiklis won an Emmy for his portrayal of Mackey, and it's easy to see why. As Mackey's lies and

---

▶ REPLAY

In 2004, after being nominated for the award five times, *The Sopranos* won the Emmy Award for Outstanding Drama Series. It would continue to be nominated every year it was eligible, winning again for its final season in 2007. Matthew Weiner, who shared the Emmy with David Chase and the other executive producers, would go on to win the award the next four years for *Mad Men*, until *Homeland* broke his winning streak in 2012.

deceptions continue to pile up, the actor does a fantastic job of keeping his character (almost) sympathetic. It's not that Mackey wants to blur the line between good and bad or right and wrong—he wants to erase it altogether. With *The Shield*, FX broke into the prestige drama landscape that had never before been occupied by a basic cable channel.

A series about a corrupt vice squad that put law-breaking cops front and center was unusual for television at the time *The Shield* premiered. Although antiheroes like Tony Soprano and the inmates of *Oz* were around, having a cop behave like a criminal was a risk. FX grew especially wary following 9/11, when law enforcement personnel were being heralded for their bravery. Their hesitations disappeared after the release of *Training Day* (2001), Antoine Fuqua's hit—and Oscar-winning—film about corrupt cop Alonzo Harris (Denzel Washington) making his own rules. Suddenly, Vic Mackey seemed more relevant than ever.

Mad Men (2007–2015)

When *Mad Men* made its television debut in summer 2007, its storyline seemed straightforward enough: When he's not creating brilliant advertising campaigns for some of the country's biggest corporations, a handsome Madison Avenue executive named Don Draper (Jon Hamm) likes to smoke, drink, and cheat on his wife—and is often aided and abetted in these activities by his boss, the equally debonair Roger Sterling (John Slattery). But as the series continues, cracks begin to show in Don's perfectly chiseled exterior, and it becomes clear that we are only beginning to scratch the surface of who, exactly, Don Draper is.

As such, *Mad Men* developed a slightly more mysterious tone as time went on—one that ultimately led devoted viewers to wonder whether the show had ever been straightforward at all, or if they had been hoodwinked. Had *Mad Men* been some sort of strange 1960s fever dream all along?

There were bizarre fan theories (a popular one was that Draper was actually the notorious hijacker D. B. Cooper) and immediate suspicion if creator Matthew Weiner dared to let the camera linger on the image of an open elevator (what's he trying to tell us?). Was there anything to this heightened sense of paranoia? The best way to answer that question is to dive into the series and find out for yourself.

Ozark (2017–2022)

Getting on the wrong side of the wrong people is a classic mistake, but Marty Byrde (Jason Bateman) went ahead and did it anyway—and dragged his family along for the ride. The Netflix series *Ozark* is a bit like *Breaking Bad* . . . if Walter White had come clean about making drugs early on, and if Skyler (in this case, Laura Linney's more-than-complicit wife, Wendy Byrde) had been completely on board.

To make the show as realistic as possible, *Ozark*'s writers needed to develop a firm understanding of how money laundering works in real life. Naturally, they called the feds. "We had an FBI agent who investigates money laundering come and sit down with us for a day so we could pick her brain," producer Chris Mundy said.

Who's the best antihero in the history of television? _____

WHY: _____

MATCH the
Mad Men character to their memorable quote:

A. Don Draper
B. Roger Sterling
C. Joan Holloway Harris
D. Pete Campbell
E. Peggy Olson
F. Betty Draper
G. Lane Pryce

___ 1. **"I'm not a solution to to your problems. I'm another problem."**

___ 2. **"People want to be told what to do so badly that they'll listen to anyone."**

___ 3. **"Am I the only one who can work and drink at the same time?"**

___ 4. **"Every time an old man starts talking about Napoleon, you know they're going to die."**

___ 5. **"You're painting a masterpiece, make sure to hide the brushstrokes."**

___ 6. **"I feel like I just went to my own funeral. I didn't like the eulogy."**

___ 7. **"Not great, Bob!"**

BLOOD WORK

Why are serial killers so fascinating? Maybe it's their ability to walk among us without ever tipping their true intentions. These fictional slashers have the added benefit of being embodied by charismatic performers.

Dexter (2006–2013; 2021)

"Homicidal" has not traditionally been a character trait jotted down by television writers in the hope of landing on a sympathetic lead. With *Dexter*, Showtime's dark—and darkly comic—drama, the writers got away with murder. Built on the considerable talent and charm of *Six Feet Under* star Michael C. Hall, and based on Jeff Lindsay's book series that began with *Darkly Dreaming Dexter*, the show asks viewers to sympathize with Dexter Morgan (Hall), a blood spatter lab technician at the fictional Miami Metro Police Department by day, and a serial killer by night.

Dexter's murderous impulses, which he can't seem to ignore, are directed at villains the world would seemingly be better off without. His detective sister Deb (Jennifer Carpenter) grounds him in a loose family unit, while a succession of love interests attempt to pull genuine emotion from Dexter's shackled heart. It's a police procedural crossed with the Grand Guignol gore shows of French theater, all of it anchored by Hall's struggle between being human and

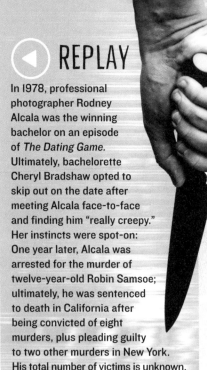

REPLAY

In 1978, professional photographer Rodney Alcala was the winning bachelor on an episode of *The Dating Game.* Ultimately, bachelorette Cheryl Bradshaw opted to skip out on the date after meeting Alcala face-to-face and finding him "really creepy." Her instincts were spot-on: One year later, Alcala was arrested for the murder of twelve-year-old Robin Samsoe; ultimately, he was sentenced to death in California after being convicted of eight murders, plus pleading guilty to two other murders in New York. His total number of victims is unknown.

indulging in his inner monster (or, as he calls it, his Dark Passenger). Vigilante ritual killings are wrong, of course, but in Hall's knife-wielding hands, we sometimes have to remind ourselves of that.

The big question of the series finale was: Would Dexter live or die? He almost died in a hurricane, but Showtime was adamant that he needed to live. "They [wouldn't] let us kill him," producer John Goldwyn said. "Showtime was very clear about that."

The finale, however, ended up being largely unsatisfying—not just for fans, but for Hall as well. In 2021, *Dexter* came back, in large part to address the many questions the finale left unanswered.

Hannibal (2013–2015)

In 2013, Bryan Fuller set about crafting a new version of the Hannibal Lecter story. It was a daring proposition after the character and his world had been so clearly defined by Sir Anthony Hopkins's performance and after Hannibal's presence in four novels and five feature films. But Fuller had an idea no one else had approached yet: He wanted to show what he described to Collider as "the bromance between Hannibal [Mads Mikkelsen] and Will Graham [Hugh Dancy]. Here are two crazy men, who are so unique in their insanity that they need each other to understand themselves." What audiences got was one of the most stylish, visually arresting, and psychologically complex shows ever to hit television.

Hannibal lasted only three seasons, but in its short time on the air, it amassed loads of critical acclaim and a ravenous fan base known as "Fannibals," many of whom are still holding out hope for the show's return.

For a show like *Hannibal*, elaborate crime scenes full of mutilated bodies were always going to be part of the process. Fuller took a very hands-on approach to craft the various gruesome murders, with the help of NBC's standards and practices department. Rather than script or shoot something and then have to fight with network censors about what he could or couldn't show, Fuller worked proactively. He reached out to the network directly with his ideas first, then worked with them to create the most NBC-friendly version of *Hannibal* possible. As a result, he learned a few tricks to get around broadcast TV's violence limitations—like that the redder and brighter the blood is, the less you can show. "So if you darken the blood and throw it into shadow, then you can be much more graphic than you normally would be able to," Fuller said.

Mindhunter (2017–2019)

We've been obsessed with serial killer fiction for many decades now, going back to at least 1955, when Patricia Highsmith made us shake hands with *The Talented Mr. Ripley*. Director David Fincher (*Se7en*) produced this unsettling Netflix drama that explores the meta-layer of that obsession by profiling the earliest days of the FBI unit that investigated serial murder.

Mindhunter centers on FBI Agent Holden Ford (Jonathan Groff), FBI Agent Bill Tench (Holt McCallany), and psychologist Wendy Carr (Anna Torv) as they build the department by conducting face-to-face interviews with human monsters. The show is based on the true crime book of the same name, co-written by famed FBI profiler John E. Douglas, so nearly every character is based on someone from real life. That also goes for the serial killers, including fictionalized versions of Ed Kemper, Charles Manson, and more, all drawn from interview transcripts. It's a delicate, gorgeous show exploring our worst impulses and, chillingly, uses real serial killers' own words to describe their acts.

You (2018–present)

Based on the book series by Caroline Kepnes, *You* strikes a precarious balance. The viewer is supposed to find stalker Joe Goldberg (*Gossip Girl*'s Penn Badgley) abhorrent, duplicitous, and likely insane. But his increasingly clever ploys to win over the unfortunate targets of his misguided affection are layered and cunning. He's a reinvention of Thomas Ripley—a character so malignant we can't help but be captivated by what line he'll cross next.

Who's a TV antagonist you can't help but love?

WHY:

BULLET POINTS

Assassins need love, too—and these series prove that there's nothing wrong with rooting for a hired killer.

Killing Eve (2018–present)

If you have yet to watch *Killing Eve*, you're missing out on one of TV's most delicious crime dramas. And spy thrillers. And black comedies. Just when you think you know where the genre-busting series about an MI5 desk drone turned field agent (Sandra Oh) helping track down a psychopathic assassin (Jodie Comer) is headed, it changes the rules—which helps explain why the show has been such a hit with audiences and critics alike.

Killing Eve is based on a series of four Kindle singles that became the novel *Codename Villanelle* by Luke Jennings, a dance critic for England's *The Observer*. In 2014, producer Sally Woodward Gentle optioned the rights to Jennings's stories about a Russian assassin (Comer's Villanelle) and an ambitious MI5 agent (Oh's Eve) who chase each other around the world in a global game of cat and mouse.

"Although the notion of a female assassin was not unique, Luke's take was fresh, intelligent, and tonally much bolder than others," Woodward Gentle said. "It wasn't exploitative. We really enjoyed the character of Villanelle and the inventiveness of her kills, but we were particularly engaged with the mutual obsession between the women."

Phoebe Waller-Bridge, who began her entertainment career as an actor before helming *Crashing* and *Fleabag*, was brought on to develop *Killing Eve* based on her work on the stage version of *Fleabag*, which she performed as a one-woman show in 2013. The material turned out to be a perfect match for the creator's sensibilities.

"I write from the point of view of what I'd like to watch," Waller-Bridge told *The Guardian* in 2018. "I'm always satisfying my own appetite. So I guess that means transgressive women, friendships, pain. I love pain."

Barry (2018–present)

When *Saturday Night Live* alum Bill Hader told TV dynamo Alec Berg (*Seinfeld, Silicon Valley*) that he wanted to make a show about a hitman, Berg thought the genre was glib and played out but was intrigued enough to see where they could take the story. When Hader told HBO he wanted to play the hitman, they responded with, "*You?*"

Yes, him. Hader has delivered another indelible comic character into our lives through *Barry*. This time it's someone who kills for a living but seeks an escape from that low-drama, high-violence world in the high-drama, low-violence world of acting class. The show is an incredible feat of tonal balance that's equally comfortable going for humor and heartache; it's something truly fresh and original, even by prestige TV standards.

The key to Barry is that he's very good at something that's bad for him. The same went for Hader, who has long been plagued by intense stage fright. "I had very bad anxiety about being onstage," Hader told Vulture about his years at *SNL*. "I also didn't like the live aspect of the show."

The flip side to Barry's unhealthy skill set is his escapist desire to dive deep into a world he doesn't have much talent for. That's an existential collision that brings about massive change, so naturally Hader turned to a movie about the personified emotions in a little girl's head for inspiration. Hader voiced Fear for Pixar's *Inside Out*, and Pete Docter's original pitch— how his daughter transformed from a joyful child to a sullen teenager—really stuck with Hader, who approached *Barry* not by starting from the joke but by considering each character's emotion.

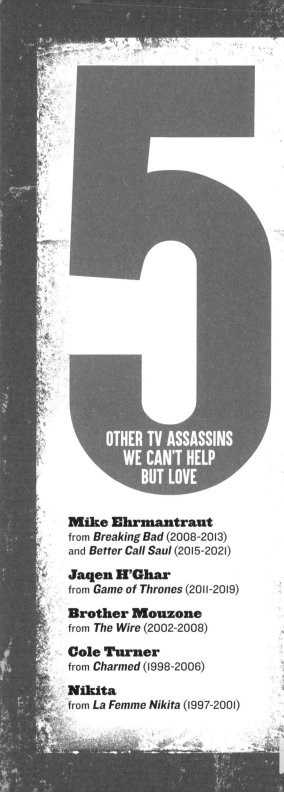

OTHER TV ASSASSINS WE CAN'T HELP BUT LOVE

Mike Ehrmantraut
from *Breaking Bad* (2008-2013)
and *Better Call Saul* (2015-2021)

Jaqen H'Ghar
from *Game of Thrones* (2011-2019)

Brother Mouzone
from *The Wire* (2002-2008)

Cole Turner
from *Charmed* (1998-2006)

Nikita
from *La Femme Nikita* (1997-2001)

Two Degrees of...
Sandra Oh

Fill in the title of the TV show or movie that connects these actors to *Killing Eve* star Sandra Oh.

DANNY TREJO
was in

_____
TV SHOW OR MOVIE NAME
(2004) with Ben Stiller, who was in

_____
TV SHOW OR MOVIE NAME
(1998) with Sandra Oh.

BENEDICT CUMBERBATCH
was in

_____
TV SHOW OR MOVIE NAME
(2016) with Susan Sarandon, who was in

_____
TV SHOW OR MOVIE NAME
(2014) with Sandra Oh.

BETTY WHITE
was in

_____
TV SHOW OR MOVIE NAME
(1999) with Bill Pullman, who was in

_____
TV SHOW OR MOVIE NAME
(2003) with Sandra Oh.

TARAJI P. HENSON
was in

TV SHOW OR MOVIE NAME
(2018) with Jane Lynch, who was in

TV SHOW OR MOVIE NAME
(2006) with Sandra Oh.

EMILIA CLARKE
was in

TV SHOW OR MOVIE NAME
(2018) with Woody Harrelson, who was in

TV SHOW OR MOVIE NAME
(2009) with Sandra Oh.

LARRY DAVID
was in

TV SHOW OR MOVIE NAME
(1987) with Dianne Wiest, who was in

TV SHOW OR MOVIE NAME
(2010) with Sandra Oh.

TV CHARACTERS I LOVE TO HATE

CHARACTER: _____

WHY: _____

_____

CHARACTER: _____

WHY: _____

_____

CHARACTER: _____

WHY: _____

_____

CHARACTER: _____

WHY: _____

_____

CHARACTER: _____

WHY: _____

_____

CHARACTER: _____

WHY: _____

_____

CHARACTER: _____

WHY: _____

_____

CHARACTER: _____

WHY: _____

_____

CHARACTER: _____

WHY: _____

_____

CHARACTER: _____

WHY: _____

_____

CHARACTER: _____

WHY: _____

_____

CHARACTER: _____

WHY: _____

_____

CHARACTER: _____

WHY: _____

_____

CHARACTER: _____

WHY: _____

Cringe Watch

The following shows may specialize in teeth-clenching awkwardness,
but that doesn't mean you'll want to look away.

Curb Your Enthusiasm **(2000–present)**
After co-creating and spending several seasons on *Seinfeld*, Larry David made himself the ultimate disruptor of acceptable behavior with *Curb Your Enthusiasm*. As "Larry David," the writer shares his on-screen alter ego's success, wealth, and tony Los Angeles zip code. But where real-life Larry and TV Larry differ is that TV Larry is a "social assassin" at large who is willing to offend and insult without a moment's hesitation. Supporting cast members J. B. Smoove, Susie Essman, Cheryl Hines, and Jeff Garlin are either co-conspirators or victims.

The show, which is mostly improvised, is clearly an outlet for the real David to give voice to the thoughts that would see him shunned if spoken out loud in the real world. "If I had my druthers, that would be me all the time, but you can't do that," David told *Rolling Stone.* "We're always doing things we don't want to do, we never say what we really feel, and so this is an idealized version of how I want to be."

Extras **(2005–2007)**
Five years after creating *The Office*, Ricky Gervais and Stephen Merchant co-created and co-starred in this series about Andy Millman (Gervais), a struggling actor who, along with his close friend Maggie Jacobs (Ashley Jensen), only ever seems to be able to land gigs as a background performer. His bumbling agent and car phone salesman Darren Lamb (Merchant) can't offer much help in the way of furthering Andy's career, which means it's up to Andy to get the TV script he's been working on into the hands of someone who matters to achieve the stardom he's always dreamed of and eventually finds (with its many trappings).

Because it's centered around the world of film and television, each episode features at least one guest star, usually a legitimate celebrity who has been enlisted to play a comically exaggerated version of themselves (like Sir Patrick Stewart, who is intent on making a movie in which he has

telekinetic powers that allow him to strip the clothes off every woman he sees, or Daniel Radcliffe as a horny teen). Gervais's "funcomfortable" style of comedy gets a full workout as his character slowly experiences a modest degree of success and then promptly squanders it, with significant help from Merchant's character, who regularly (though unintentionally) sabotages Gervais's career.

The Mindy Project (2012–2017)

Originally called *It's Messy*, *The Mindy Project* follows OB/GYN Mindy Lahiri (Mindy Kaling) and her quirky co-workers as they try to balance their professional and personal lives. The relationships on

REPLAY

As the creator, executive producer, writer, and star of *The Mindy Project*, Mindy Kaling was the first woman of color to run and star in her own network show. Kaling's TV career may have been predestined: She was named after Pam Dawber's character in *Mork & Mindy*.

The Mindy Project were directly influenced by those on *The Office*, according to Kaling. She explained her thought process in a chat with *Entertainment Weekly*: "In *The Office* were Jim and Pam, characters that are so deeply good and in many ways don't have a ton of flaws. But they were so compatible that in many ways maybe their personalities overlapped with each other's. And I love that *Much Ado About Nothing*, passionate, smart fighting. I love fighting with guys, and that's something that I don't get to see: arguing at a high level with a member of the opposite sex."

The role of her love interest Danny Castellano was written for Chris Messina, who Kaling knew through *The Office*'s John Krasinski. Kaling has said she "[finds] him so watchable. One of the highlights of this whole process is working with him. He's like an old-fashioned movie star, so appealing and masculine."

MATCH THE FICTIONAL AFFLICTION TO THE TV SHOW:

____ 1. Groat's Syndrome   A. *Doctor Who*

____ 2. Bliss Virus   B. *Curb Your Enthusiasm*

____ 3. Amoria Phlebitis   C. *True Blood*

____ 4. Hepatitis V   D. *The Office*

____ 5. Spontaneous Dental Hydroplosion   E. *The Simpsons*

Is there a television show that is too painfully cringey for you to watch?

_____

_____

WHY: _____

_____

_____

_____

_____

SERIOUS SATIRE

Satire is the sitcom's outrageous cousin—and the family member everyone wants to spend time with.

30 Rock (2006–2013)

Inspired by Tina Fey's tenure as head writer for *Saturday Night Live*, *30 Rock* is about the production of a fictional sketch series set at NBC's real-life headquarters at 30 Rockefeller Plaza in New York City. In addition to Fey's award-winning portrayal of Liz Lemon, *30 Rock* stars *SNL* alum Tracy Morgan as comedian Tracy Jordan and frequent *SNL* host Alec Baldwin as network executive Jack Donaghy.

For viewers who have never seen an episode of *Saturday Night Live*, *30 Rock* still has a lot to offer. The show helped make Fey's surreal brand of comedy instantly recognizable. Though characters like Jane Krakowski's attention-seeking Jenna Maroney and Jack McBrayer's optimistic (and possibly immortal) Kenneth Parcell are larger than life, they're also easy for audiences to love. Critics had plenty of love for *30 Rock* as well: The series earned twenty-two Emmy nominations in 2009 alone—a record for a comedy in a single year.

Fey originally pitched a show like HBO's *The Newsroom*, about a news program with a Bill O'Reilly–like host in which she'd play the producer and (in an ideal world) Alec Baldwin would play the pundit. But an NBC exec suggested she use her time at *SNL* as inspiration. Initially, she wasn't into the idea—until she thought about casting Tracy Morgan. (It didn't hurt that they had the blessing of *SNL* creator Lorne Michaels, who was an executive producer on *30 Rock*.)

Portlandia (2011–2018)

Before there was *Portlandia*, there was ThunderAnt—a comedy partnership between longtime *SNL* player Fred Armisen and Sleater-Kinney band member Carrie Brownstein, who began filming short comedy bits with recurring characters, some of whom eventually migrated to *Portlandia* (i.e., feminist bookstore owners Toni and Candace). But *Portlandia*, which debuted on IFC

▶ REPLAY

Portlandia's Women and Women First feminist bookstore sketches were shot at an actual feminist bookstore in Portland called In Other Words. Before the store closed in June 2018, it was the only nonprofit feminist bookstore in the country. The set designers left the store almost completely untouched for the show—with the exception of the books themselves. Since the show doesn't have the rights to the store's real books, production designer Tyler Robinson replaced them with fake books he created.

on January 21, 2011, allowed the duo to amplify the surreality of what they were creating, and to do so on the grander stage of a major cable network known for its offbeat programming.

Portlandia is an ode to Portland, Oregon, where the entirety of the series was shot, and it's also inspired by the city's uniquely quirky vibe. Most of the extras used on the show are local actors, and many of the show's characters are based on real Portland locals. For example, Sam Adams, the former mayor of Portland, appeared in four episodes of the show—not as the mayor of Portland,

which he actually was at the time, but as the assistant to actor Kyle MacLachlan's unnamed mayor. The show also shoots its city hall scenes in the actual Portland City Hall, and MacLachlan used Adams's actual bicycle in many of his scenes.

The title is obviously a play on the city's name, but it's also the title of a prominent statue by sculptor Raymond Kaskey that is located outside the Portland Building in the city's downtown area. You can see the statue—the country's second-largest copper repoussé sculpture (only the Statue of Liberty is bigger)—in the show's opening credit sequence.

RECASTING: 30 ROCK

30 Rock is being rebooted and it's your chance to play the casting director. Who are you hiring to play each of the key roles?

Liz Lemon _____

Jack Donaghy _____

Tracy Jordan _____

Jenna Maroney _____

Kenneth Parcell _____

Pete Hornberger _____

Frank Rossitano _____

Cerie Xerox _____

Toofer Spurlock _____

Criss Chros _____

SHOW: _____

WHY: _____

SHOW: _____

WHY: _____

SHOW: _____

WHY: _____

SHOW: _____

WHY: _____

SHOW: _____

WHY: _____

SHOW: _____

WHY: _____

SHOW: _____

WHY: _____

SHOW: _____

WHY: _____

SHOW: _____

WHY: _____

SHOW: _____

WHY: _____

SHOW: _____

WHY: _____

SHOW: _____

WHY: _____

SHOW: _____

WHY: _____

SHOW: _____

WHY: _____

SHOW: _____

WHY: _____

SHOW: _____

WHY: _____

SHOW: _____

WHY: _____

SHOW: _____

WHY: _____

SHOWS THAT MADE ME LAUGH OUT LOUD

PAPER PRODUCTS

You'd never want a boss like David Brent or Michael Scott in real life. But watching others suffer through the workday with them? Sign us up!

The Office (UK 2001–2003) vs. The Office (US 2005–2013)

If your only experience with *The Office* is via NBC's long-running American adaptation of the BBC series, you're missing out. While the original series falls firmly into the "comedy" genre, it's that very specific—and unnerving—brand of cringe comedy (think *The Larry Sanders Show* or *Curb Your Enthusiasm*) that separates the series from its more straightforward comedy competitors. And when it comes to the fine art of awkward comedy, there's no more talented practitioner than Ricky Gervais.

Whereas Dunder Mifflin's Michael Scott (Steve Carell) is more of a well-meaning social misfit who just wants to be liked, Wernham Hogg's David Brent (Gervais) is a self-centered jerk who regularly tries, and desperately fails, to command respect from those around him in the most ridiculous ways possible. And when things don't go Brent's way, he unleashes the childish beast that lurks inside him, which generally leads to some of the series' finest moments. His attempt to out-dance his immediate superior, who has everything David wants, is the kind of thing you'll have to rewind and rewatch— if only to prove that paper sales rep Tim Canterbury (Martin Freeman) has the perfect facial response to every situation.

Greg Daniels's American adaptation initially looked a lot like the UK version. But over the course of its nine-season run, *The Office* carved out its own comedic path to become in the 2000s what *Friends* was in the 1990s: the ultimate comfort food of a sitcom. Michael Scott may not be the world's best boss (despite what his coffee mug says), but he sure makes for a lovably cringe-worthy one. With a slew of "that's what she said" jokes and human resources violations, Scott maintains his position as ringleader of the wacky inner workings of the Dunder Mifflin Paper Company in Scranton, Pennsylvania, while his underlings—Dwight Schrute (Rainn Wilson), Jim Halpert (John Krasinski), and Pam Beesly (Jenna Fischer), to name a few—practically perfected the deadpan stare as they regaled the fake mockumentary crew with their own takes on the office's daily shenanigans.

In addition to the UK and America, *The Office* has made its way onto television screens worldwide. More than eighty countries have broadcast the original series, from Canada to Australia. The series has also been adapted for audiences around the world. Among the international updates are versions in France (*Le Bureau*), Germany (*Stromberg*), Canada (*La Job*), Chile (*La Ofis*), Israel (*HaMisrad*), and Sweden (*Kontoret*).

MATCH *THE OFFICE* CHARACTER TO THEIR DUNDIE AWARD:

____ 1. Jim   A. Tight-Ass Award

____ 2. Pam   B. Spicy Curry Award

____ 3. Stanley   C. Hottest in the Office

____ 4. Phyllis   D. Don't Go in There After Me

____ 5. Angela   E. Whitest Sneakers Award

____ 6. Kevin   F. Extreme Repulsiveness Award

____ 7. Ryan   G. Grace Under Fire Award

____ 8. Kelly   H. Bus(h)iest Beaver Award

____ 9. Meredith   I. Best Dad

____ 10. Toby   J. Fine Work Award

Which *The Office* character would you most like to have as a co-worker?

WHY:

Which *The Office* character would you hate to be sent to The Annex with?

WHY:

Two Degrees of...
John Krasinski

Fill in the title of the TV show or movie that connects these actors to *The Office* star John Krasinski.

JAMES GANDOLFINI
was in

_____
TV SHOW OR MOVIE NAME
(2012) with Michael Imperioli, who was in

_____
TV SHOW OR MOVIE NAME
(2012) with John Krasinski.

VIOLA DAVIS
was in

_____
TV SHOW OR MOVIE NAME
(2008) with Meryl Streep, who was in

_____
TV SHOW OR MOVIE NAME
(2009) with John Krasinski.

AWKWAFINA
was in

_____
TV SHOW OR MOVIE NAME
(2019) with Zach Galifianakis, who was in

_____
TV SHOW OR MOVIE NAME
(2011) with John Krasinski.

TIMOTHÉE CHALAMET
was in

TV SHOW OR MOVIE NAME
(2015) with Steve Martin, who was in

TV SHOW OR MOVIE NAME
(2009) with John Krasinski.

DEV PATEL
was in

TV SHOW OR MOVIE NAME
(2012) with B.J. Novak, who was in

TV SHOW OR MOVIE NAME
(2017) with John Krasinski.

 REPLAY

John Krasinski is known for his perfect comedic timing now, but his early work didn't portend that. In 2004, one year before he began giving sideways glances to the documentary crew of *The Office*, Krasinski was the anti-Jim Halpert when he played a violent—and possibly homicidal—high school basketball player facing off against Vincent D'Onofrio on *Law & Order: Criminal Intent*. Roles on *CSI: Crime Scene Investigation* and *Without a Trace* followed.

KALEY CUOCO
was in

TV SHOW OR MOVIE NAME
(2014) with Simon Helberg, who was in

TV SHOW OR MOVIE NAME
(2006) with John Krasinski.

Un-Real Estate

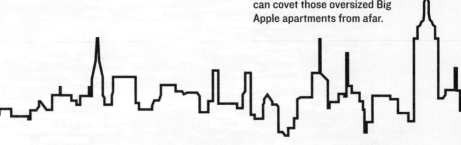

Let's face it: Living like the characters in your favorite TV series probably isn't ever going to happen. But you can covet those oversized Big Apple apartments from afar.

The Marvelous Mrs. Maisel
(2017–present)

Fans of *The Marvelous Mrs. Maisel* may fantasize about traveling back in time to live in Midge's apartment—but even in 1950s New York, the place wasn't exactly affordable. The building isn't a real location (Midge gives a fictional address in the pilot), but the set is based on a real Upper West Side apartment building: The Strathmore, originally built in 1909, is a 48-unit high-rise on Riverside Drive. Based on recent sales numbers, an apartment similar to Midge's seven-room flat would go for about $6.5 million today.

Sex and the City
(1998–2004)

For the entire original run of *Sex and the City*, Carrie Bradshaw (Sarah Jessica Parker) lived in a very chic apartment in a rent-controlled Upper East Side brownstone located on East 73rd Street between Park and Madison Avenues. Swanky, right? Too bad it was doubly fictional: Carrie's building number was 245 (a nonexistent number that, if it did exist, would be located farther east between Second and Third Avenues) and the exterior shots were actually filmed on Perry Street in the West Village—though the building's owners have since blocked off the stoop so that fans of the HBO series (and movies and series reboot) will stop using their home as a photo op.

Friends (1994–2004)

When they're not hanging out at Central Perk, the BFFs at the center of *Friends* can most often be found hanging out in their enormous (and obviously rent-controlled) apartments. When *Friends* first began, Monica (Courteney Cox) and Rachel (Jennifer Aniston) lived in apartment number 5. When producers later realized that didn't make sense, as they lived on a higher floor, they changed their apartment number to 20. The number on Joey (Matt LeBlanc) and Chandler's (Matthew Perry) apartment changed as well—from 4 to 19.

3 TV HOMES YOU CAN VISIT

HIGHCLERE CASTLE //
Downton Abbey

LOCATION:
HAMPSHIRE, ENGLAND

In addition to its iconic exterior, the library, dining room, drawing room, and grand hallway featured on *Downton Abbey* all belong to Highclere Castle, the real-life home to the Earl and Countess of Carnarvon, which is open to visitors several times throughout the year (and occasionally offers overnight stays).

ROSEBUD MOTEL //
Schitt's Creek

LOCATION:
ORANGEVILLE, ONTARIO, CANADA

You don't need to lose your video store fortune to wind up at the Rosebud Motel. It may have been the Rose family's last resort, but fans of *Schitt's Creek* eagerly flock to to what was officially known as the Hockley Motel, which hit the market for $1.6 million in 2021.

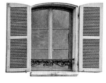

DOUNE CASTLE //
Game of Thrones & Outlander

LOCATION:
DOUNE, SCOTLAND

Fantasy fans will recognize this medieval fortress from two epic series: It served as *Game of Thrones*'s Winterfell and *Outlander*'s Castle Leoch.

My Dream TV Show Homes Would Be:

_____

_____

_____

_____

WIT'S END

A dramedy is a delicate balancing act, and these ones do it perfectly.

Fleabag (2016–2019)

In just two short seasons, *Fleabag* made a lasting mark on television that won't soon be forgotten. Phoebe Waller-Bridge's darkly hilarious series follows Fleabag, a thirty-something Londoner—played by the effortlessly funny Waller-Bridge—who is caught up living a life of late nights filled with booze and promiscuity in the wake of her mother's death. At first, *Fleabag* appeared to be a simple half-hour comedy following the often-naughty exploits of its quirky main character. But as the series progressed, it quickly proved itself to be a truly masterful piece of work, with each episode adding more complicated layers and darker themes to which many viewers could relate.

Witty and frank about sensitive topics (e.g., sex, death, and "losing the currency of youth"), the character quickly became the impulsive alter ego of millennial viewers who saw aspects of their own messy, disillusioned lives depicted on-screen. Season two introduced an additional reason to watch in the form of Irish actor Andrew Scott (*Sherlock*) as a sweary, irreverent (and nameless) cleric whom the internet zealously christened "Hot Priest." Though fans clamored for more, Waller-Bridge's multiple Emmy wins ended up being *Fleabag*'s de facto finale. "This just feels like the most beautiful, beautiful way to say goodbye to it," she said after the awards ceremony. "It does feel nice to go out on a high. You can't get higher than this."

The title *Fleabag* comes from a nickname given to Waller-Bridge by her family. Speaking to *This Morning* in April 2020, the series creator and star (who is also responsible for bringing *Killing Eve* to the small screen) revealed a deeper meaning for the name choice, which is never actually spoken in the show. "A fleabag motel is something that's a bit rough around the edges," she explained. "I wanted to call her that because I wanted her persona and her outside aesthetic to give the impression that she was completely in control of her life, when actually, underneath, she's not."

I May Destroy You (2020)

I May Destroy You is a kaleidoscopic investigation into the aftermath of trauma, a celebration and indictment of the power of social media, and a radical meditation on empathy. The title is as much a warning to viewers as it is the name of this limited series created, written, produced by, and starring Michaela Coel (who won a BAFTA for her previous series, *Chewing Gum*, in 2016). Any attempt to summarize the series in just a few words would be reductive; it's best to enter the show with as little information as possible, as much of its power rests in the sum total of the entire viewing experience and the way it kicks around in your brain for days, if not weeks, afterward.

The series begins with Arabella (Coel)—a social media star who writes a best-selling book called *Chronicles of a Fed-Up Millennial* and is currently struggling with finishing her second book—going out for a night with friends that ends with Arabella blacking out. The next morning, flashes of the night come back to her, and Arabella realizes she was the victim of a violent sexual assault that she can only remember in pieces. So rather than finish her new book, which her agents and publisher are waiting for, Arabella sets out on a journey to piece together the evening and figure out who was responsible, while also using her platform as the voice of a generation to rally others around her cause.

I May Destroy You is about much more than the attack that kicks off the series. It's an exploration of the concept of consent (or, as is often the case, the lack thereof), the murkiness surrounding rape culture, and what it takes to rebuild one's life in the aftermath of trauma. The story is semi-autobiographical for Coel—who is mesmerizing to watch—which makes it

REPLAY

Michaela Coel wrote 191 drafts of *I May Destroy You*. It paid off: The show, which was the most critically acclaimed series of 2020, according to Metacritic, earned Coel a slew of awards, including several BAFTAs and Independent Spirit Awards, as well as an Emmy, a Peabody, and an NAACP Image Award.

even more personal and effective. But her greatest achievement may very well be that, through all the pain, Coel still somehow manages to imbue the script with her trademark humor, making *I May Destroy You* one of the most surprising, stylish, frank, discomfiting, challenging, and ultimately satisfying series to come along in a long time. Incisive and surprising, it will leave you sure of nothing but Coel's prodigious talent.

What TV series plot twist did you *not* see coming?

_____

_____

_____

_____

_____

_____

_____

_____

_____

_____

_____

_____

_____

Two Degrees of...
Mindy Kaling

Fill in the title of the TV show or movie that connects these actors to *The Mindy Project* star Mindy Kaling.

DANNY DEVITO
was in

_____
TV SHOW OR MOVIE NAME
(1994) with Emma Thompson, who was in

_____
TV SHOW OR MOVIE NAME
(2019) with Mindy Kaling.

CILLIAN MURPHY
was in

_____
TV SHOW OR MOVIE NAME
(2010) with Joseph Gordon-Levitt, who was in

_____
TV SHOW OR MOVIE NAME
(2015) with Mindy Kaling.

NORMAN REEDUS
was in

_____
TV SHOW OR MOVIE NAME
(2015) with Michael Peña, who was in

_____
TV SHOW OR MOVIE NAME
(2018) with Mindy Kaling.

JUNO TEMPLE
was in

TV SHOW OR MOVIE NAME
(2014) with Dennis Haysbert, who was in

TV SHOW OR MOVIE NAME
(2012) with Mindy Kaling.

KIT HARINGTON
was in

TV SHOW OR MOVIE NAME
(2018) with Natalie Portman, who was in

TV SHOW OR MOVIE NAME
(2011) with Mindy Kaling.

KERRY WASHINGTON
was in

TV SHOW OR MOVIE NAME
(2013) with Craig Robinson, who was in

TV SHOW OR MOVIE NAME
(2005-2013) with Mindy Kaling.

SHOWS THAT MADE ME CRY FOR DAYS

All in the Family

No two families are alike, but that doesn't mean you can't see
part of your own in your favorite on-screen clans.

Modern Family (2009-2020)

When TV veterans Christopher Lloyd and
Steven Levitan brought *Modern Family* into
the world on September 23, 2009, people
weren't quite sure what to expect. Though
it featured a sprawling cast of actors, only
Ed O'Neill (a.k.a. *Married . . . with Children*'s
Al Bundy) was a household name, at least
at the time. But with its whip-smart writing
and talented cast of comedic actors, *Modern
Family* became an awards magnet, winning
the Emmy for Best Comedy Series an
impressive five years in a row.

Jay Pritchett (O'Neill), the family
patriarch, is remarried to a much younger
woman named Gloria (Sofía Vergara), who
has a son named Manny (Rico Rodriguez)
from her previous marriage. Jay's daughter,
Claire (Julie Bowen), and her real estate
agent husband, Phil Dunphy (Ty Burrell),
have three children—Haley (Sarah Hyland),
Alex (Ariel Winter), and Luke (Nolan
Gould)—while Jay's son, Mitchell (Jesse
Tyler Ferguson), and his husband, Cameron
(Eric Stonestreet), have one child, their
adopted daughter, Lily (Aubrey Anderson-
Emmons for most of the show's run).

Why are the Dunphys and Pritchetts
always talking to the camera? There's no
reason given, but originally the show had
one. *Modern Family* was initially conceived
as a documentary shot by Geert Floortje,
a Dutch filmmaker who had lived with the
Pritchetts as a teenage exchange student and
had come back to the United States as an
adult to film them. But Geert got cut before
Modern Family entered production because,
according to Levitan, his documentarian
openings, closings, and interview questions
"risked becoming an appendage that you
had to serve every week." The show was
simply shot documentary-style, without
the fictitious camera crew.

Black-ish (2014–present)

Black-ish could have easily been yet another
toothless, trope-filled network sitcom about
an upper-middle-class family. Instead, it
has become a work of important social
significance that isn't afraid to tackle the
issues facing Black families in America
today. Anthony Anderson and Tracee Ellis
Ross have received a ton of accolades for
their roles as Dre and Rainbow Johnson,
a couple who are worried their kids are
losing touch with their Black culture.

Though the series has been critically acclaimed since its premiere, its second season took the show's message even further and tackled everything from racial slurs to police brutality. Now several seasons in, *Black-ish*'s social conscience sees it regularly compared to *Good Times, A Different World*, and other pioneering series before it. It has also launched the spin-offs *Grown-ish*, *Mixed-ish*, and *Old-ish*, with each series speaking to a distinct audience.

When *Black-ish* debuted in 2014, there was a big discussion about its title and what it meant. Show creator Kenya Barris told NPR that it's a reflection of his anxieties about raising his children in a more privileged world than he knew as a kid. "I wanted to be honest with what it's like sort of raising your kids in a different environment than you were accustomed to being raised in," he explained. "My kids are nothing like I remember Black kids being when I was a kid."

When *Black-ish* executive producer–star Laurence Fishburne was asked about the show's title on *The View*, his explanation was blunter: "For some people, it means when Black folks kind of act white. For some people, it means when white folks kind of act Black . . . I think of it this way. Two words: Justin Bieber.

Justin Bieber acts 'Black-ish,' but he doesn't get shot by the police. He gets a police escort home."

Fresh Off the Boat (2015–2020)

Inspired by chef Eddie Huang's 2013 memoir of the same title, Nahnatchka Khan created this comedy series, narrated by Huang in season one, about a Taiwanese-American family in 1990s Florida. Randall Park (*Always Be My Maybe*) and Constance Wu (*Crazy Rich Asians*) play parents to three children who relocate to Orlando to open a cowboy-themed steak house and bring Randall's mother (Lucille Soong) along for the ride.

Huang withdrew his involvement in the series after the first season and was upfront about his issues with the show—namely, that the network took a very specific story about life in America and broadened the comedy and storylines for a mass-market audience. "The network tried to turn *Fresh Off the Boat* into a cornstarch sitcom, and me into a mascot for America," Huang wrote in *New York Magazine*. "I hated that. This show isn't about me, nor is it about Asian America. The network won't take that gamble right now."

Still, the show received numerous awards for its writing and performances. And though the series ran for six seasons, most of them without Huang's involvement, Huang called *Fresh Off the Boat* "a gateway [to Asian-American culture]," adding: "I don't watch it, but I'm proud of what it does."

MATCH THE DOG TO THE TV SHOW:

_____ I. Eddie   A. *Full House*

_____ 2. Comet   B. *Gilmore Girls*

_____ 3. Stella   C. *WandaVision*

_____ 4. Paul Anka   D. *Frasier*

_____ 5. Sparky   E. *Modern Family*

Which TV family can you relate to the most?

WHY:
_____
_____
_____

DRAWN TOGETHER

Dysfunctional families, crass humor, and sharp satire
separate these animated series from the
Saturday morning toons you watched as a kid.

The Simpsons
(1989–present)

The Simpsons has been a television institution for more than thirty years. Since its debut on Fox in 1989, the series has accumulated a mountain of awards, worldwide acclaim, and an empire of merchandise—not to mention so many episodes that it would take more than two full weeks to binge-watch all of it in one session. But if you're looking to make a long-term commitment to a show that's smart, funny, and surprisingly heartfelt, this is the perfect series to have in your queue.

Homer, Marge, Lisa, Bart, and Maggie Simpson may be the stars, but *The Simpsons* is just as much about its robust ensemble. The number of memorable recurring characters in Springfield is made even more impressive by the fact that they're all voiced by a handful of well-respected actors like Hank Azaria, Harry Shearer, and many others, who make up a kind of repertory theater company of amazing voice talent.

A *Simpsons* episode can become a cultural event, as was the case in figuring out who shot Mr. Burns—there was no shortage of suspects—or finally hearing Maggie's first word ("Daddy"). The show is even considered prescient, seemingly predicting everything from the infamous tiger attack against magician duo Siegfried and Roy to a pro soccer corruption scandal. The folks behind *The Simpsons* are smart. *Incredibly* smart. One look through the writers and producers who

MATT GROENING

TM & © 2002 FOX

have passed through the show reveals graduates, scholars, and professors from some of the best universities on the planet. And many of them didn't start out by studying writing. Al Jean, who has been the showrunner since 2001, began studying mathematics at Harvard when he was just sixteen. Writer Jeff Westbrook was an algorithm researcher and attended both Harvard and Princeton before becoming an associate professor at Yale. Writer David X. Cohen graduated from Harvard with a physics degree and the University of California, Berkeley with a computer science degree. And this is just a sample of the brainpower it takes to bring *The Simpsons* to life. American satire has never been drawn so beautifully.

Family Guy
(1999–present)

Unless you abstain from television entirely, it's likely you've caught at least a few minutes of the hit animated series *Family Guy*. The show centers on the Griffin family: parents Peter and Lois; children Meg, Chris, and Stewie; and their talking dog, Brian. While it's considered an iconic series today, it didn't get off to the most promising start. Most fans know the story of the show's early cancellation and subsequent revival after massive DVD sales and rerun ratings convinced Fox to give it another shot. This comes as no surprise, as *Family Guy* has regularly been the center of a larger conversation—from the show's many controversies over its ruthless satire, to its Emmy Awards, to its undeniable influence over today's pop culture.

Creator Seth MacFarlane first pitched *Family Guy* to Fox around the same time that Mike Judge was signing a deal for *King of the Hill*. Uncertain of how *King of the Hill* would fare with viewers, Fox executives were hesitant to add another new animated comedy to their lineup. Because of this, they decided to pass on *Family Guy*.

One year later, MacFarlane followed up with Fox to see if *Family Guy* was still dead in the water. As it turned out, the success of *King of the Hill* was a key factor in Fox's decision to take on another new animated comedy. They gave MacFarlane $50,000 to create an episode; he spent six months creating a seven-minute pilot, which was enough to convince the network to order thirteen *Family Guy* episodes to air in mid-season. It was a key development that made Fox the clear leader in prime time animation from the 1990s to today.

Which animated TV family would you rather be a part of—the Simpsons or the Griffins? _____

WHY: _____

_____

MATCH *The Simpsons* quote to the character who said it:

A. Homer Simpson
B. Bart Simpson
C. Marge Simpson
D. Lisa Simpson
E. Ned Flanders
F. Milhouse Van Houten
G. Moe Szyslak
H. Ralph Wiggum
I. Nelson Muntz
J. Kent Brockman

___ 1. **"I, for one, welcome our new insect overlords."**

___ 2. **"You don't win friends with salad."**

___ 3. **"Everything's coming up Milhouse."**

___ 4. **"Me fail English? That's unpossible."**

___ 5. **"I don't want to alarm anybody, but I think there's a little al-key-hol in this punch."**

___ 6. **"I'm better than dirt. Well, most kinds of dirt."**

___ 7. **"Spend less time on your back and more time on your knees."**

___ 8. **"Shoplifting is a victimless crime. Like punching someone in the dark."**

___ 9. **"Pablo Neruda said, 'laughter is the language of the soul.'"**

___ 10. **"I didn't think it was physically possible, but this both sucks and blows."**

RICHE$ TO RAGS

A family's fall from grace is never something to laugh at—unless it's one of these families.

Arrested Development (2003–2019)

This smart, snarky series follows the irreverent story of the Bluths, a dysfunctional Orange County family that loses their real estate fortune after the SEC begins investigating the family business for fraud. After the family patriarch, George Bluth Sr. (Jeffrey Tambor), goes to prison, his son Michael (Jason Bateman) is left to grudgingly hold the family together.

Arrested Development was adored by critics for its intricate running jokes and dense humor—but executives at Fox weren't always laughing, especially when ratings began to slip. In 2014, Hurwitz told an audience at the Banff World Media Festival that the network feared the show was too complicated for viewers; following season two, he received a note from Fox executives to "dumb it down" by 25 percent—yes, they gave him an exact number. Hurwitz recalled that when he told executives he would only make the show his way, he was told, "You can make it, but we'll basically just make your life miserable."

Arrested Development's intricately crafted plotlines, recurring gags, and relentlessly clever wordplay earned the adoration of a cult following, but it didn't drive ratings high enough to keep Fox from canceling the show after its third season. Still, the show's producers—along with the series' die-hard fans—wouldn't let *Arrested Development* go down without a fight. In 2013, seven years after being axed by Fox, the Bluth family was revived on Netflix for a fourth season, followed by a fifth in 2018, proving yet again that there's always money in the banana stand.

Schitt's Creek (2015–2020)

If you've enjoyed Catherine O'Hara and Eugene Levy in any of their past film roles as an oddball couple, you won't be let down by *Schitt's Creek*. After they lose their entire video store fortune to the government because their business manager hasn't been paying their taxes, the Rose family—parents Johnny (Levy) and Moira (O'Hara) and their adult children, David (Daniel Levy, Eugene's son) and Alexis (Annie Murphy)—head to the only asset the government has allowed them to keep: the rural town of Schitt's Creek, which Johnny once purchased as a joke. The cosmopolitan Roses move into the local motel, where they share two adjoining rooms.

Schitt's Creek is a classic fish-out-of-water story,

REPLAY

The ten-room Hockley Motel in Mono, Ontario is located about fifty miles northwest of Toronto and played the role of the Rosebud Motel on *Schitt's Creek*. In addition to *Schitt's Creek*, the property has served as a filming location for Netflix's *The Umbrella Academy*, Hulu's adaptation of Stephen King's *11.22.63*, and David Cronenberg's 2005 thriller *A History of Violence*.

but at its heart is a show about family. Though the series, which originally aired on Pop TV, struggled to find its audience in the first few seasons (largely because most people had never heard of Pop TV), all of that changed when *Schitt's Creek* arrived on Netflix and benefited from what is known as the "Netflix bump." In 2020, *Schitt's Creek* made TV history when it swept all seven major comedy categories at the Emmys, and Daniel Levy became the first person to win all four major Emmy categories (producing, writing, directing, and acting) in a single year.

To flesh out his idea for *Schitt's Creek*, Daniel Levy turned to his dad, comedy icon Eugene. The two had never worked together before; in fact, pre-*Schitt's*, Daniel had been adamant about doing his own thing. Daniel explained to NPR that he went to his dad with this idea because he had seen the family-loses-it-all idea "played out on mainstream television and sitcoms, but I'd never really seen it explored through the lens of a certain style of realist comedy that my dad does so well. So I came to him and pitched the idea and asked him if he would be interested at all in just fleshing it out and seeing if there was anything there."

Eugene and Daniel weren't the only Levys on the show, either. Sarah Levy, daughter of Eugene and sister of Daniel, also appeared on *Schitt's Creek* as Twyla Sands, the lone waitress at the town's most happening diner, Café Tropical.

MATCH THE RECURRING *ARRESTED DEVELOPMENT* CHARACTER TO THE ACTOR WHO PLAYED THEM:

___ 1. Barry Zuckerkorn	A. Julia Louis-Dreyfus
___ 2. Lucille Austero	B. Ed Begley Jr.
___ 3. Tony Wonder	C. Isla Fisher
___ 4. Cindi Lightballoon	D. Liza Minnelli
___ 5. Stan Sitwell	E. Ben Stiller
___ 6. Kitty Sanchez	F. Charlize Theron
___ 7. Rita Leeds	G. Henry Winkler
___ 8. Rebel Alley	H. Martin Mull
___ 9. Gene Parmesan	I. Judy Greer
___ 10. Maggie Lizer	J. Jane Lynch

Which TV family is most like your own?

HOW SO: _____

Two Degrees of...
Catherine O'Hara

Fill in the title of the TV show or
movie that connects these actors to
Schitt's Creek star Catherine O'Hara.

ALEXANDER SKARSGÅRD
was in

_____
TV SHOW OR MOVIE NAME
(2014) with Meryl Streep, who was in

_____
TV SHOW OR MOVIE NAME
(2004) with Catherine O'Hara.

GEORGE TAKEI
was in

_____
TV SHOW OR MOVIE NAME
(2016) with Charlize Theron, who was in

_____
TV SHOW OR MOVIE NAME
(2019) with Catherine O'Hara.

PHOEBE WALLER-BRIDGE
was in

_____
TV SHOW OR MOVIE NAME
(2011) with Richard E. Grant, who was in

_____
TV SHOW OR MOVIE NAME
(2006) with Catherine O'Hara.

BLAKE LIVELY
was in

TV SHOW OR MOVIE NAME
(2010) with Ben Affleck, who was in

TV SHOW OR MOVIE NAME
(2004) with Catherine O'Hara.

BILL HADER
was in

TV SHOW OR MOVIE NAME
(2009) with Harold Ramis, who was in

TV SHOW OR MOVIE NAME
(2002) with Catherine O'Hara.

TRACEE ELLIS ROSS
was in

TV SHOW OR MOVIE NAME
(2009) with Jessica St. Clair, who was in

TV SHOW OR MOVIE NAME
(2006) with Catherine O'Hara.

THE ONE PERCENT

Billionaires: They're not like us! But finding out exactly how is endlessly entertaining in the form of cleverly written TV.

Billions (2016–present)

At a time when the widening wealth gap in America is a frequent topic of conversation, *Billions* is the perfect show about godlike financial power and our complicated feelings for those who wield it. The show follows one such powerhouse: billionaire hedge fund manager Bobby "Axe" Axelrod (Damian Lewis), who uses his street smarts, country-sized fortune, and guts of steel to take down rivals and carve out an even larger piece of the pie for himself. Not everything he does is legal, which is how he earns the ire of US Attorney for the Southern District Chuck Rhoades (Paul Giamatti), who is married to world-class performance coach Wendy Rhoades (Maggie Siff). Since the show loves its complications, Wendy just happens to work for Axelrod.

Over the course of several seasons, the show has evolved from a game of cat-and-cat between two egomaniacs using their power and influence against each other to an expansive view of the players oozing in and out of the global financial market. Alliances are

REPLAY

Both *Billions* and *Succession* employ "wealth consultants," who help advise the production on how the richest of the rich live. Kieran Culkin told *Variety* about the time the *Succession* cast filmed a shot getting out of a helicopter and were given some notes about it. "They told us, 'You would have been doing this your whole lives. You know where the propeller is. You wouldn't be ducking your head.'"

MATCH THE TV SHOW TO ITS TAGLINE:

_____ 1. *Billions*   A. Misery just found company

_____ 2. *Succession*   B. Justice has a price

_____ 3. *Fargo*   C. Every hero has a code

_____ 4. *Dead to Me*   D. Power is the ultimate currency

_____ 5. *Game of Thrones*   E. Aw, jeez, here we go again

_____ 6. *Westworld*   F. Take what's yours

constantly shifting, breaking, and reforming because theirs is a world of transaction and vengeance that lasts only until a partnership can be profitable enough to erase any bad blood.

Billions gets a lot right. Co-creators and co-show-runners Brian Koppelman and David Levien work with their cast tirelessly to make sure that even the smallest details help build authenticity and heft. But their track record isn't perfect: According to Koppelman, a billionaire wrote them to praise the show's dedication to real gilded life, but mentioned he "would never be caught dead flying in the sardine can of a plane [they] put Axe into." This isn't unusual when playing in the sandbox of the ultrarich, especially as so many of them are fans of the show. As Koppelman noted, only a billionaire would think of a G5 as a "starter plane."

Succession
(2018–present)

The antics of the dysfunctional Roy family—the fictional-but-Murdoch-like owners of Waystar Royco, an international media and hospitality conglomerate—are at the center of HBO's dark satire *Succession*. Ever since the series debuted in 2018, it has captivated audiences and critics alike. With its sharp scripts and carefully composed characters, *Succession* is utterly compelling television. But as the brainchild of Jesse Armstrong—co-creator of British hits *Peep Show* (2003–2015) and *Fresh Meat* (2011–2016), and a writer on *The Thick of It* (2005–2012)—the show is also bitingly funny.

While a dysfunctional family drama doesn't seem like a natural environment for improvisation, the actors are given great freedom to ad-lib while filming. The cast will shoot their scripted scenes, then do other takes where creativity is encouraged. According to Nicholas Braun, who plays "Cousin Greg" Hirsch, he and his fellow cast members "improv in probably every scene to some capacity." For example, the scene in the pilot where the characters are at the dinner table was apparently entirely improvised. Also improvised? Kendall Roy's (Jeremy Strong) iconic meltdown in the bathroom after finding out his father has betrayed him.

Speaking of Strong: It's almost impossible to mention Kendall without acknowledging his rap tribute to his father, Logan (Brian Cox), in *Succession*'s season two episode "Dundee." While the rap itself was scripted (written by the show's composer, Nicholas Britell), the characters' hilarious reactions were not. Strong told *Entertainment Weekly*, "I worked on it incessantly, and then asked our director, Kevin Bray, 'Can we shoot them seeing it for the first time as well as me doing it for the first time?' So their responses, which are the best part of it, are genuine." It's worth rewatching the scene a few times to truly appreciate the range of reactions.

Which TV show has the best opening title sequence?

WHY:

_____

_____

_____

_____

Girls' Trips

Girl power rules on these TV series.

Gilmore Girls (2000–2007)

For viewers with a high tolerance for caffeine and fast talking, *Gilmore Girls* presents an idyllic slice of small-town New England life. Lorelai Gilmore (Lauren Graham) is an unconventional single mom who defected from her upper-crust upbringing after getting pregnant at sixteen. Her daughter, Rory (Alexis Bledel), is much more studious and soft-spoken, but she shares her mother's love of coffee and pop culture.

Just as loveable as the main mother-daughter duo is the show's robust ensemble, which includes the quirky residents of the town of Stars Hollow, Lorelai's wealthy and out-of-touch parents, and Rory's and Lorelai's numerous love interests. *Gilmore Girls* introduced us to creator Amy Sherman-Palladino's rapid-fire brand of humor, which she has since re-created in *Bunheads* and *The Marvelous Mrs. Maisel*. But to fans of her first show, no characters have exemplified the art of gab quite like the Gilmores.

The show was inspired by a trip Sherman-Palladino took through the small town of Washington, Connecticut. "We're driving by, and people are slowing down saying, 'Excuse me, where is the pumpkin patch?'" she recalled. "And everything is green and people are out, and they're talking. And we went to a diner and everyone knew each other and someone got up and they walked behind the [counter] and they got their own coffee because the waitress was busy." Within twenty-four hours, Sherman-Palladino had worked out the show and written some of the pilot's dialogue.

Girls (2012-2017)

Lena Dunham created the Judd Apatow–produced *Girls*, which explores the lives of a group of women living in New York and the serio-comic travails of their young lives, as a rejoinder to the wish-fulfillment fantasies of series like *Sex and the City*.

Broadcast between 2012 and 2017, the show lasted six seasons and featured Dunham, Allison Williams, Jemima Kirke, Zosia Mamet, and a revolving door of up-and-coming semi-regular actors, including Adam Driver and Andrew Rannells, who made their first impressions on audiences in memorable supporting roles.

Despite its legacy as a platform for so many talented performers, the show received criticism for its too-frequent exclusion of non-white voices and perspectives. Though Dunham expressed regret over the lack of diversity, she told *NYLON* magazine, "When I wrote the pilot I was 23. Each character was an extension of me. I thought I was doing the right thing. I was not trying to write the experience of somebody I didn't know, and not trying to stick a Black girl in without understanding the nuance of what her experience of hipster Brooklyn was."

REPLAY

Oscar nominee Adam Driver was catapulted to fame by Lena Dunham's *Girls,* but he initially passed on even auditioning for the series, as he wasn't interested in doing TV. He told Vulture that his original thought was "TV's the devil . . . but then I read the thing. Lena is a very rare writer, very unpretentious." Driver ended up playing Adam Sackler for all six seasons of the critically acclaimed series.

Good Girls (2018-2021)

Off the Map and *Scandal* co-creator Jenna Bans is responsible for this effervescent comedy series about three mothers in suburban Michigan who enter into a life of crime after deciding to rob a supermarket to make ends meet. Christina Hendricks (*Mad Men*), Retta (*Parks and Recreation*), and Mae Whitman (*Arrested Development*) play the three leads, who harbor different feelings about their criminal activities as they navigate the advantages and ethical repercussions of their financial windfall.

Though *Good Girls* was canceled after four seasons, it developed a small but strong following as it explored the daily lives of suburban women with a delightfully incisive sense of humor. Meanwhile, the show baked in a number of Easter eggs for vigilant viewers, such as the fact that both Beth (Hendricks) and Ruby (Retta) always drank from the same coffee cup in every episode.

If someone were to make a TV series based around you and your best friends, what would the title be?

Who would play you?

FAMILY AFFAIRS

If you've ever dreamed of running a family business,
these shows might have you questioning that decision.

It's Always Sunny in Philadelphia (2005-present)

The friends-just-hanging-out trope had been well established in sitcoms by the time *It's Always Sunny in Philadelphia* premiered in 2005. So had the notion that characters could be selfish narcissists (see *Seinfeld*). But *Sunny* had one advantage over Jerry and his crew of misfits: It was on basic cable, and network standards of decorum didn't apply.

From its earliest seasons, the crew at Paddy's Pub has been able to mine humor from the most depraved of situations (for proof, just look at episode titles like "The Gang Finds a Dumpster Baby"). Virtually none of the characters have any redeeming qualities. Ringleader Dennis Reynolds (series co-developer Glenn Howerton) is a sociopath who may or may not have killed in the past; twin sister Dee Reynolds (Kaitlin Olson) suffers from self-delusion over her talents; guileless Charlie Kelly (series co-developer Charlie Day) is prone to

huffing gasoline; Mac (series creator and co-developer Rob McElhenney) volleys from heavyset to super-fit in a pinball of self-image issues; and Frank Reynolds (Danny DeVito), father(ish) figure to Dennis and Dee, has allowed his advancing years to remove any veneer of empathy from his actions.

These are all terrible people, prone to scheming, scamming, and exploiting others or themselves in the misplaced ambition to get ahead, and viewers have connected with their depravity. In 2020, FX renewed *Sunny* for a fifteenth season, making it the longest-running live-action comedy series in the history of television. Eventually—though not too soon—the

◀ REPLAY

Rob McElhenney, Glenn Howerton, and Charlie Day were relatively unknown when they spent less than $100 to produce a pilot called *It's Always Sunny on TV*, about struggling actors competing for the role of a cancer patient. After shopping it around, they found a buyer in FX. For the proper pilot, the setting was changed to the fictional Paddy's Pub, an Irish dive bar in Philadelphia, and *It's Always Sunny in Philadelphia* was born.

MATCH THE FATHER TO THE TV SHOW:

____ 1. Phil Dunphy   A. *This is Us*

____ 2. Jack Pearson   B. *Riverdale*

____ 3. Michael Kaye   C. *Gossip Girl*

____ 4. Fred Andrews   D. *Modern Family*

____ 5. Cyrus Rose   E. *My Wife and Kids*

Gang Will Close Its Doors. Very few lessons will have been learned. Fans wouldn't have it any other way.

Bob's Burgers (2011–present)

Created by Loren Bouchard of *Dr. Katz, Professional Therapist* and *Home Movies* fame, *Bob's Burgers* follows the burger-slinging Belcher family—parents Bob and Linda, and their three rambunctious children, Tina, Gene, and Louise—as they struggle to run the family's hamburger joint.

Much like the early days of its fellow animated series *Family Guy*, *Bob's Burgers* has earned its place in Fox's "Sunday Funday" lineup not through breakout ratings but with the unwavering support of its dedicated fan base. Like Bouchard's previous work, *Bob's Burgers* has amassed a large cult following, thanks in part to the show's memorable catchphrases (can't you just hear Tina's groan or Linda's "Alright" in your head?), its ridiculous (yet hilariously catchy) tunes, and its many, many guest stars, including Emmy winner Jon Hamm as a talking toilet.

When Bouchard first pitched the idea of *Bob's Burgers* to Fox, he had a slightly different vision for the family that fans know and love today. He imagined the Belchers as cannibals, with their restaurant serving as a cover for their dietary habits. "There was a brief period when I first started talking to [the network executives]—because I was coming off of doing *Lucy: Daughter of the Devil* and I had this kind of more occult-y, sort of darker edge to the way I was thinking then," Bouchard told The A.V. Club. "I did pitch the show [as] a family of cannibals who run a restaurant." While the network chose to steer Bouchard away from the cannibalism concept, he did incorporate that idea into the pilot episode in the form of Louise spreading a rumor that the family's burgers were, in fact, made of human flesh.

What is the best pilot episode of all time?

_____

WHY: _____

MY FAVORITE RECURRING CHARACTERS OF ALL TIME

CHARACTER: _____

SHOW: _____

CHARACTER: _____

SHOW: _____

CHARACTER: _____

SHOW: _____

CHARACTER: _____

SHOW: _____

CHARACTER: _____

SHOW: _____

CHARACTER: _____

SHOW: _____

CHARACTER: _____

SHOW: _____

CHARACTER: _____

SHOW: _____

CHARACTER: _____

SHOW: _____

CHARACTER: _____

SHOW: _____

CHARACTER: _____

SHOW: _____

CHARACTER: _____

SHOW: _____

CHARACTER: _____

SHOW: _____

CHARACTER: _____

SHOW: _____

CHARACTER: _____

SHOW: _____

CHARACTER: _____

SHOW: _____

CHARACTER: _____

SHOW: _____

CHARACTER: _____

SHOW: _____

CHARACTER: _____

SHOW: _____

CHARACTER: _____

SHOW: _____

The ROYAL TREATMENT

From England to Russia, women make the rules in these royally impressive shows.

The Crown
(2016–present)

When Netflix first announced its plans to produce *The Crown* in 2014, all viewers really knew was that they were getting a ten-episode series based on Peter Morgan's play *The Audience*, which revolved around Queen Elizabeth II's weekly meetings with the prime minister. Several seasons later, *The Crown* has become one of the most ambitious, most lauded projects in the history of streaming—and daring in its decision from the get-go to regularly replace its main actors as the characters grow older. So while the series kicked off with Claire Foy and Matt Smith playing the roles of the queen and Prince Philip, they were replaced by Olivia Colman and Tobias Menzies in season three, who were then replaced by Imelda Staunton and Jonathan Pryce in season five.

Morgan's sweeping epic is set against a truly opulent backdrop (Netflix has spared no expense when it comes to recreating historic places like Buckingham Palace) and has as much to offer history lovers as it does royal enthusiasts. Its extravagances aside, the show is brought to life by the best and brightest actors Britain has to offer. But *The Crown*'s real genius lies in the way it makes every small moment a massively memorable one: the single tear shed by the queen (Colman) after visiting the Aberfan mining disaster zone, or Margaret Thatcher's (Gillian Anderson) fish-out-of-water facial expression as she tries to hold her own during a goofy parlor game at Balmoral Castle. The cumulative result is a surprisingly human portrait of the Windsors and all their affiliates that exists somewhere between a history textbook and a tabloid headline.

The road to *The Crown* started with *The Deal*, a 2003 TV movie starring Michael Sheen about former prime minister Tony Blair's rise to power. *The Queen* was a continuation of that story, focusing on a newly elected Blair (played again by Sheen) working to push the queen to take action in the wake of Princess Diana's death. That led to *The Audience*, a play that opened in London in 2013 and eventually made its way to Broadway. In 2016, when asked by *Variety* why he wanted to tell the story of the queen's rise to power, Morgan's response was honest: "I didn't really. I'm sick of writing the world of Elizabeth. But when we did the play *The Audience*, the scene between [Winston] Churchill and the young queen struck me as having lots of potential."

Victoria (2016–present)

While *The Crown* may nab the bigger headlines, *Victoria*—the *Masterpiece* series that similarly follows a young and not-quite-ready royal's ascension to England's throne—beat Netflix's pricey TV series to the air by more than two months. And though it was originally intended as a one-off miniseries, the gorgeous, Buckingham Palace–set period piece about the early days of Queen Victoria's reign kept getting renewed.

In order to better help her get into the mindset of her character, *Victoria* star Jenna Coleman was given access to Queen Victoria's private diaries. "I've read so many biographies, but I'm always looking for certain details which give me access to her character and her psychology," Coleman told Vulture in 2017. "Her diaries are so methodological in a lot of ways. You can find out what she ate for breakfast and what time she did this and what time she rose and what time she did everything. The detail is crazy."

While Victoria was a trendsetter in many ways (she is frequently the person credited with making white wedding dresses the standard), her varying interests also might have foretold today's true crime obsession. While going through her personal papers, Coleman learned that Victoria was completely fascinated by Jack the Ripper. Following the death of Mary Jane Kelly, the Ripper's final victim, Victoria contacted the prime minister and urged him to employ better detectives. (Coincidentally, at one point, Queen Victoria's own grandson, Prince Albert Victor, Duke of Clarence and Avondale, was briefly a suspect.)

The Great (2020–present)

Hulu's *The Great* is proof that a show about eighteenth-century history doesn't have to feel dull, stuffy, or unrelatable—especially if it doesn't focus too much on historical accuracy. Created by Tony McNamara, this so-called "occasionally true story" follows Catherine the Great (Elle Fanning) as she navigates her crummy marriage to Russian emperor Peter III (Nicholas Hoult) and eventually pulls the throne out from under him in a somewhat smooth coup.

With quirky characters, quippy dialogue, and equal heaps of style and satire, *The Great* is more than a little reminiscent of 2018's *The Favourite*. This isn't altogether a coincidence: McNamara also co-wrote the screenplay for that Oscar-winning film.

REPLAY

The adorable Cavalier King Charles Spaniel that plays Queen Victoria's most trusted four-legged BFF, Dash, in *Victoria* has some experience with the role. The pup, whose name is Tory, made her acting debut playing Dash in Jean-Marc Vallée's 2009 movie *Young Victoria*, starring Emily Blunt and Rupert Friend.

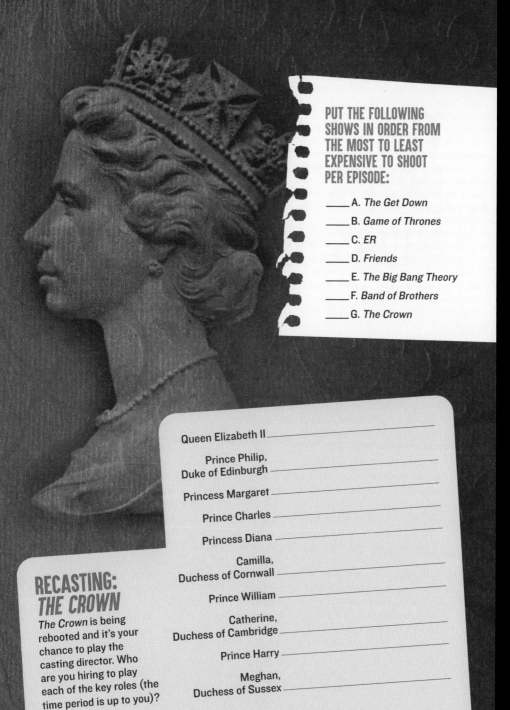

PUT THE FOLLOWING SHOWS IN ORDER FROM THE MOST TO LEAST EXPENSIVE TO SHOOT PER EPISODE:

_____ A. *The Get Down*

_____ B. *Game of Thrones*

_____ C. *ER*

_____ D. *Friends*

_____ E. *The Big Bang Theory*

_____ F. *Band of Brothers*

_____ G. *The Crown*

RECASTING: THE CROWN

The Crown is being rebooted and it's your chance to play the casting director. Who are you hiring to play each of the key roles (the time period is up to you)?

Queen Elizabeth II _____

Prince Philip, Duke of Edinburgh _____

Princess Margaret _____

Prince Charles _____

Princess Diana _____

Camilla, Duchess of Cornwall _____

Prince William _____

Catherine, Duchess of Cambridge _____

Prince Harry _____

Meghan, Duchess of Sussex _____

THE BRITISH INVASION

Pour a hot cuppa and head back in time to England of yesteryear.

Downton Abbey (2010–2015)

The *Upstairs, Downstairs*–like balance between the dramas that faced early twentieth-century aristocrats Robert (Hugh Bonneville) and Cora Crawley (Elizabeth McGovern)—aka the Earl and Countess of Grantham—and the troubles of their trusty servants downstairs made *Downton Abbey* a completely addictive watch. And the show's impeccable attention to detail, thanks in large part to historical advisor Alastair Bruce, made shooting the show a rather expensive endeavor. According to *The World of Downton Abbey*, each episode cost about $1.5 million to produce.

In keeping with the show's dedication to authenticity, the producers maintained a "no-wash" policy with some of the costumes, including those belonging to some of the kitchen workers', in order to keep within the period look—which meant the actors could get a little stinky. "They have these weird patches, which are sewn into the armpits and which they wash separately," Sophie McShera (kitchen maid–turned–assistant cook Daisy) told *Daily Mail*.

Call the Midwife (2012–present)

Originally inspired by Jennifer Worth's memoirs about her time working as a nurse and midwife in London's East End, the show dives into the gritty details of daily life in London's Poplar neighborhood during the 1950s and 1960s. Midwives, working with the nuns of Nonnatus House, zip around the city's postwar East End, delivering babies and treating all sorts of medical ailments, with a dash of their own intimate dramas added to the mix.

To ensure a certain level of realism, *Call the Midwife* has a trained midwife to coach actors through the scenes. "I have taught the actors how to take blood pressure or listen to a baby's heartbeat through a pregnant abdomen using a Pinard [stethoscope] correctly using the equipment," Terri Coates, the show's midwife advisor, told the BBC.

But Coates's connection to the material goes even deeper: It was an article Coates had written for the journal *Royal College of Midwives* that originally inspired Worth to write her own stories.

"Jennifer said that she had always planned to write in her retirement and that my article provided the catalyst for her memoirs," Coates told the BBC.

Poldark (2015-2019)

This all-new version of the vintage *Masterpiece* series stars Aidan Turner as Captain Ross Poldark, a British redcoat returning to Cornwall after the American Revolutionary War, only to find that nothing is the same. In addition to the death of his father, Ross learns that Elizabeth (Heida Reed), the love he left behind, is now engaged to his close-as-a-brother cousin Francis Poldark (Kyler Soller). As time passes, Ross moves on and finds an even deeper love with his one-time scullery maid, Demelza (Eleanor Tomlinson). The series is based on Winston Graham's book series, which included a total of twelve novels written between 1945 and 2002.

While *Poldark* is a British production through and through, the same can't be said for the show's sprawling cast. Turner is Irish, while Soller was born in Connecticut. Perhaps most surprisingly, partly because she intentionally uses an English accent in interviews, Reed is Icelandic; her given name is Heiða Rún Sigurðardóttir.

RECOMMENDED BINGE-WATCHING: BRITISH PERIOD DRAMAS

Period dramas can be addictive. From the carefully curated costumes and set designs to the colorful language and turns of phrase, it's easy to get caught up in the old-timey details of a great series that takes you back in time. Here are five more of them.

1. *The Forsyte Saga* (2002-2003)
2. *The Tudors* (2007-2010)
3. *Upstairs, Downstairs* (2010-2012)
4. *Sanditon* (2019-present)
5. *The Great* (2020-present)

If you could spend a day going back in time to live in one period drama, which show would you choose?

WHY:

REPLAY

During World War I, Almina Herbert, 5th Countess of Carnarvon, turned Highclere Castle—the three-hundred-room Hampshire estate where much of *Downton Abbey* was shot—into a recovery hospital for soldiers. Art then imitated life when the Crawleys turned their home into a convalescent home for soldiers.

ERA PRONE

Romance and adventure come together in engrossing, and unexpected, ways in these period pieces.

Outlander (2014–present)

In 2014, Starz debuted *Outlander*, a historical drama that defies easy categorization (unless historical time travel romantic drama is, indeed, already a genre). Based on Diana Gabaldon's beloved and best-selling book series—which itself was influenced by an episode of *Doctor Who*—the show is centered on military nurse Claire Randall (Caitriona Balfe) who, following the end of World War II, takes a second honeymoon with her husband, Frank (Tobias Menzies), to Scotland . . . where she tumbles through some Scottish standing stones that transport her from 1945 to 1743. In the past she meets—and marries—Jamie Fraser (Sam Heughan), a Highlander with strong values and stronger muscles.

Though Claire is the central figure in the series, Balfe was only offered the role of Claire a few weeks before filming began. "At the outset, I told everyone that we would find Claire first and then Jamie would be the last one cast, and of course

REPLAY

In traditional Scottish fashion, the actors on *Outlander* aren't wearing anything beneath their kilts. "I'm a true Scotsman, and . . . one of the joys of working on the show is wearing the kilt," Sam Heughan, who plays Jamie Fraser, told *Entertainment Weekly*. "It can actually be very comfortable."

it was exactly the opposite," showrunner Ronald D. Moore told *E! News.* "Sam came in really early in the process and he was literally the first one we cast. We saw the tape and we were like, 'Oh my god, there he is. Let's snatch him up now.' And then Claire just took a long time. A lot of actresses, a lot of tape, looking for really ineffable qualities. She had to be smart, she had to have a strength of character, and really, she had to be someone that you could watch think on camera. But then suddenly Caitriona's tape came in and we had that same light bulb moment."

Bridgerton (2020–present)

On Christmas Day 2020, Netflix audiences were introduced to the deliciously lavish (and sometimes naughty) existence of the Bridgerton family, originally brought to life in Julia Quinn's series of historical romance novels. The debut season follows the events of *The Duke and I*, the first book in the series, in which the eldest Bridgerton daughter, Daphne (Phoebe Dynevor), sets out to find a husband in 1813.

Over the course of both the show and the book, Daphne meets Simon Basset (Regé-Jean Page), the Duke of Hastings, and they strike a deal: They pretend to be courting so that Simon can stop being pestered by eager mothers trying to marry their daughters off to an eligible duke. In return, Daphne can attract more suitors by making them jealous. What could go wrong? A lot, it turns out.

Though Netflix is notoriously tight-lipped about its viewing statistics, the streamer was so optimistic about *Bridgerton*'s potential for success that they publicly predicted that approximately 63 million homes would have watched *Bridgerton* in its first month of release. On January 27, 2021, Deadline announced that *Bridgerton* had already been viewed by 82 million households, making it Netflix's biggest original hit ever (previously, the top spot had belonged to *The Witcher*, which got 76 million views in its first month). Perhaps even more impressive is that the show has held the top spot on Netflix's Top 10 in seventy-six different countries— so it's not surprising that Netflix went ahead and renewed *Bridgerton* for another three seasons.

Which TV couple do you consider relationship goals?

_____

&

_____

MATCH THE FICTIONAL ESTATE TO ITS TV SERIES:

_____ 1. Haxby Park   A. *Poldark*

_____ 2. Winterfell Castle   B. *Peaky Blinders*

_____ 3. The Shelby Parlour   C. *Outlander*

_____ 4. Castle Leoch   D. *Downton Abbey*

_____ 5. Nampara   E. *Game of Thrones*

MY FAVORITE
TV Show Couples

_____ & _____

_____ & _____

_____ & _____

_____ & _____

_____ & _____

_____ & _____

_____ & _____

_____ & _____

_____ & _____

_____ & _____

SWORD PLAY

Gone are the days when loving all things medieval and magical got you labeled a loser for life. These series have helped make high fantasy hot.

Game of Thrones (2011–2019)

Based on *A Song of Ice and Fire*, the fantasy book series by George R. R. Martin, *Game of Thrones* is a brilliantly realized epic detailing a power struggle that pits various factions against one another for the fate of the mysterious land of Westeros. Multiple plot threads are woven together to form a tapestry of violence, deception, and infighting, with a colorful army of characters that will either delight or disgust you (or maybe a bit of both). Though it ended up being one of the biggest shows of all time, it didn't start out that way: An original unaired pilot was so poorly received that it had to be scrapped entirely and reshot.

The *Game of Thrones* cast features breakout performances by Peter Dinklage (Tyrion Lannister), Emilia Clarke (Daenerys Targaryen), Kit Harington (Jon Snow), Maisie Williams (Arya Stark), Sophie Turner (Sansa Stark), and Lena Headey (Cersei Lannister). Be cautious, however, about getting too attached to any of the show's characters—author George R. R. Martin

REPLAY

Henry "Superman" Cavill had to hustle to earn his role as Geralt of Rivia in *The Witcher*. As a fan of the books and games, he started campaigning for the part before showrunner Lauren Schimdt Hissrich had even written the pilot. Schmidt Hissrich thought he was annoying, but she met with Cavill anyway—then couldn't get him out of her head as she was writing. They auditioned 206 actors before circling back to the annoying guy who already knew he was the perfect witcher.

and showrunners David Benioff and D. B. Weiss had no problem killing off even the most beloved figures vying for control of the Iron Throne.

In a behind-the-scenes featurette, longtime *Game of Thrones* camera operator Sean Savage shared that his very favorite scene to film over eight seasons was the moment during the Battle of the Bastards "when Jon Snow is forced to the ground and then trampled. And this seemingly immortal hero of ours looks like he's close to the end." When Harington fell to the ground, Savage stood over him and filmed from above as tons of stuntmen piled on top of the actor. The scene wasn't entirely scripted, so in order to ensure that Harington wouldn't be injured, "we had a sort of safe word

[so] that we could call it off at any point," Savage said. It was surely a decision that Harington, who played Snow, appreciated; he has previously discussed how difficult that scene was for him because he is claustrophobic and "mortally afraid of crowds."

Even if you're not a fan of high fantasy, the familial struggles and blockbuster action should be more than enough to keep you hooked on *Game of Thrones* until the very end.

The Witcher (2019–)

Polish author Andrzej Sapkowski's fantastical book series about a monster hunter was a monster hit for Netflix, becoming the most-watched first season of an original series at the time of its release (until *Bridgerton* came along). The show follows the witcher Geralt of Rivia (Henry Cavill), a magical hunter of grotesque monsters whose destiny is tied to Princess Ciri (Freya Allen) but who keeps regularly running into sorceress Yennefer of Vengerberg (Anya Chalotra) because of a spell. It all adds up to a TV series that is both schlocky and intense and the kind of show one might call a "guilty pleasure." Plus, as the worm in your ear probably knows, it comes with a killer soundtrack.

Just as *Game of Thrones* became a televised hit years after its source material was first published in 1996, *The Witcher* was birthed from a short story written more than thirty years before the show came about. Author Andrzej Sapkowski wrote "Wiedźmin" ("The Witcher") as an entry for speculative fiction magazine *Fantastyka*'s annual contest (he won third place); he then wrote three more stories that were ultimately published as a collection in 1990, and he released two more collections in 1992 and 1993. The first novel was released in 1994, and the video game adaptation didn't hit the scene until 2007. It's been a long road with a big return.

The Lord of the Rings (2022)

Inspired by, but not to be confused with, either of Peter Jackson's film series *The Hobbit* or *The Lord of the Rings*, this Amazon Prime series explores many of the characters that audiences fell in love with on the silver screen but at a different time—thousands of years earlier, during the Second Age of Middle-earth.

Since it's been a while in the making, the show arrives more in the wake of the success of *Game of Thrones* than J. R. R. Tolkien's theatrical epics, but early images indicate that Jackson's films have provided a visual template for Middle-earth that likely will not change as filmmakers like J. A. Bayona (*Jurassic World: Fallen Kingdom*) explore its violent complexities.

Nevertheless, producers J. D. Payne and Patrick McKay seem to have created a show that takes its cues from the ideas and tone of Tolkien's creation rather than the letter of his literature— and apparently did so successfully; the show is fully produced with the cooperation of the iconic author's estate.

MATCH the quote to the *Game of Thrones* character who said it:

A. Daenerys Targaryen

B. Tyrion Lannister

C. Lord Petyr Baelish

D. Sansa Stark

E. Jon Snow

F. Arya Stark

___ 1. **"The lone wolf dies but the pack survives."**

___ 2. **"Fear cuts deeper than swords."**

___ 3. **"It's hard to put a leash on a dog once you've put a crown on its head."**

___ 4. **"All men must die, but we are not men."**

___ 5. **"Chaos isn't a pit. Chaos is a ladder."**

___ 6. **"Love is the death of duty."**

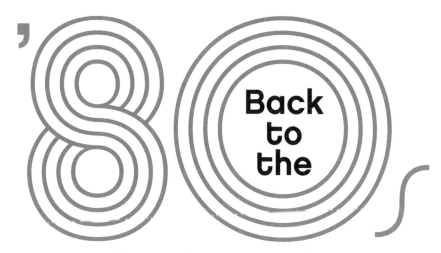

Back
to
the

Throw on some leg warmers, set the tracking,
and take a trip back in time to the decade of excess.

GLOW (2017–2019)

Anchored by wonderfully heartfelt performances by Alison Brie (Ruth "Zoya the Destroya" Wilder), Betty Gilpin (Debbie "Liberty Belle" Eagan), and a stellar ensemble cast, *GLOW* follows a group of women who star in a wrestling show that's backed by trust fund kid Sebastian "Bash" Howard (Chris Lowell) and cranky cult horror director Sam Sylvia (Marc Maron). It scored laughs for how awkward everything was early on, but the show really sailed when Brie and her cohorts began to fully own the weird, wonderful spandex assault they were creating.

The series is based on the very real Gorgeous Ladies of Wrestling, which was organized in 1986, and strikes a perfect balance between comedy and drama amid dozens of different personalities all seriously trying to find themselves in an activity no one takes seriously.

Like her character, Brie got rejected a lot before getting the role, enduring a grueling casting process for producers and a casting director who wanted an unknown for the part. "I cried in my car after every audition," she told IndieWire. "I would sit in my car like Ruth and sob. And we were both listening to the same *Ultimate 80s* mix while [we] audition[ed], so Flock of Seagulls was playing."

On September 20, 2019, Netflix announced that *GLOW* had been renewed for a fourth and final season. One year later, in the midst of the COVID pandemic,

ALISON BRIE HAS LENT HER VOICE TO MANY HIT ANIMATED PROGRAMS. WHICH SHOW HAVE YOU *NOT* HEARD HER ON?

____ 1. *BoJack Horseman*

____ 2. *Rick and Morty*

____ 3. *American Dad*

____ 4. *Family Guy*

____ 5. *Robot Chicken*

Netflix reversed its decision and canceled the series due to production shutdowns.

Pose (2018-2020)

Not long after its 2018 premiere, *Pose* began making history. The series, which dramatizes New York City's underground drag ball scene of the late 1980s and early 1990s, was co-created by Steven Canals and über-showrunners Ryan Murphy and Brad Falchuk. Like so many of their other series, *Pose* puts representation at the forefront of the show. Without ignoring the hardships facing its characters—many of whom would be relegated to the margins of other shows—*Pose* brings to life a unique culture full of joy and perseverance and has been heartily embraced by viewers and critics.

Pose is a very different sort of project for Murphy (co-creator of *Glee, American Horror Story, Scream Queens*, and *The Politician*) and one that he wanted to use in order to give back to the LGBTQ+ community. "I'm not showrunner here, I'm an advocate for this community," Murphy told *The Hollywood Reporter*, "and my job is to take care of them and provide for them and to give them access into a mainstream world that they have been denied for so long."

While the gender identities of real-life ballroom performers ranged widely and defied easy categorization, contestants in the femme queen competition category were primarily transgender women. With well over one hundred trans actors and crew members, from star Indya Moore to writer-producer Janet Mock, *Pose* sets a new standard for telling compelling stories about trans people—especially in the way it recognizes that no person can be reduced to a single label.

Which series from the 1980s still hold up today?

_____

_____

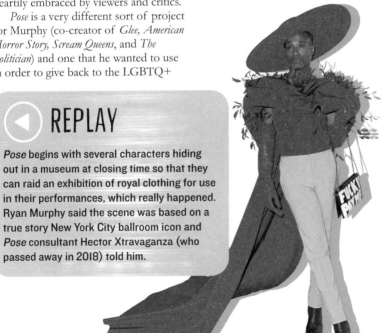

◁ REPLAY

Pose begins with several characters hiding out in a museum at closing time so that they can raid an exhibition of royal clothing for use in their performances, which really happened. Ryan Murphy said the scene was based on a true story New York City ballroom icon and *Pose* consultant Hector Xtravaganza (who passed away in 2018) told him.

Representation is a powerful force with these series that broke new ground in television.

Transparent (2014-2019)

All the major streaming networks seem to have that one breakout hit. For Amazon Studios, it was Joey Soloway's *Transparent*. On February 6, 2014, Amazon began streaming the series' pilot, and both viewers and critics were immediately smitten. By the time the show's first full season debuted on September 26, 2014, viewers had fallen madly in love with the Pfeffermans, a difficult family trying to make sense of their lives in the wake of their father (Jeffrey Tambor) coming out as a trans woman named Maura. A slew of awards—BAFTA and Emmys included—followed, making *Transparent* Amazon's first series to win a major award and the first streaming series to win a Golden Globe for Best Television Series. But *Transparent* wasn't just a triumph for Amazon; it also broke new ground for trans representation.

Producer Rhys Ernst told *OUT* that he felt strongly about casting a trans actor to portray a young Maura (Tambor) in season three's flashback sequences, ultimately hiring twelve-year-old Sophia Grace Gianna (who had recently transitioned) for the part.

This trans-inclusiveness was part of *Transparent*'s DNA. Ernst said that the show employed more than fifty trans and gender-nonconforming people in the capacity of "crew members or as actors with speaking roles." That doesn't include what he estimates to be "hundreds of extras."

Unfortunately, like the dysfunction surrounding the Pfeffermans, there was trouble brewing on the *Transparent* set. In late 2017, at the same time the show's fifth season was being written, word spread that Tambor had been hit with two sexual harassment claims from people close to the series. On November 19, 2017, Tambor quit the show; on February 15, 2018, Tambor was officially fired. And on September 27, 2019, *Transparent*'s final episode—a musical finale that took the place of a fifth

season—aired, thus bringing the series to a close. While the turmoil led to a reckoning for Tambor, there's no denying that the show (and his character in particular) left a powerful imprint on the many viewers it touched.

Insecure (2016–2021)

For more than a decade, Issa Rae has been busy carving out a unique space for Black female voices in Hollywood. It began with *Awkward Black Girl*, her witty YouTube web series, which grew up to become *Insecure*, the Emmy Award–winning HBO series Rae co-created with TV veteran Larry Wilmore.

In addition to being one of the show's creators, Rae is also its star. She plays *Insecure*'s Issa Dee, a like-minded albeit fictional version of herself who works at a nonprofit organization aimed at helping Black teens. With the help of her best friend, Molly (Yvonne Orji), a corporate lawyer whose professional success is in direct contrast to her romantic track record, Issa does her best to argue against there being "a universal way to be Black." The result is a painfully authentic portrait of the early days of adulthood through the eyes of two young Black women—a perspective not often seen on television, and one that has attracted some mega-star

directors, including Debbie Allen, Kerry Washington, and Oscar winner Regina King.

Each season of *Insecure* has included a show within the show that both the characters and the viewers enjoy, from the forbidden romance soap *Due North*, inspired by a writers' room joke, to *Kev'yn*, a spoof on nineties TV sitcoms and recent nostalgic reboots. Season four featured the mockumentary series *Looking for Latoya*, a satirical look at the ways that missing Black women are often ignored. It was such a hit they created a fictional podcast episode.

Reservation Dogs (2021–present)

Bear (D'Pharoah Woon-A-Tai), Elora (Devery Jacobs), Willie Jack (Paulina Alexis), and Cheese (Lane Factor) are bored with living in the small, low-income town of Okern and ready to escape to the wild wonders of California. They've been saving money by pulling off slightly-more-than-petty crimes, like stealing and selling a food truck, and trying to duck the attention of the town cop (Zahn McClarnon) and the paintball gun–toting NDN Mafia.

This FX show from Taika Waititi and Sterlin Harjo may be a newcomer, but it's already making a name for itself for its number of firsts. In addition to being the first series to be shot entirely in Oklahoma, *Reservation Dogs* features a creative team comprised of Indigenous artists and takes great joy in subverting or goofing on stereotypes. Less than a month after airing its pilot on August 9, 2021, the series was renewed for a second season.

WHICH EMMY-WINNING SKETCH SHOW IS ISSA RAE AN EXECUTIVE PRODUCER ON?

_____ 1. *Saturday Night Live*

_____ 2. *The Amber Ruffin Show*

_____ 3. *I Think You Should Leave*

_____ 4. *A Black Lady Sketch Show*

_____ 5. *Drunk History*

What's a show-within-a-show you'd like to actually watch?

_____

_____

SHOWS TO RECOMMEND

SHOW: _____

TO: _____

SHOW: _____

TO: _____

SHOW: _____

TO: _____

SHOW: _____

TO: _____

SHOW: _____

TO: _____

SHOW: _____

TO: _____

SHOW: _____

TO: _____

SHOW: _____

TO: _____

SHOW: _____

TO: _____

SHOW: _____

TO: _____

SHOW: _____

TO: _____

SHOW: _____

TO: _____

SHOW: _____

TO: _____

SHOW: _____

TO: _____

SHOW: _____

TO: _____

SHOW: _____

TO: _____

SHOW: _____

TO: _____

SHOW: _____

TO: _____

SHOW: _____

TO: _____

SHOW: _____

TO: _____

Pocket Protectors

Geek chic is the name of the game, and the recipe for some fantastic television.

The Big Bang Theory (2007–2019)

Sitcom veterans Chuck Lorre and Bill Prady created *The Big Bang Theory*, which premiered on CBS on September 24, 2007. The comedy followed nerdy Caltech physicist roommates Sheldon Cooper (Jim Parsons) and Leonard Hofstadter (Johnny Galecki), who befriend their non-scientist neighbor Penny (Kaley Cuoco). For twelve seasons, the gang—which also included Howard Wolowitz (Simon Helberg), Rajesh Koothrappali (Kunal Nayyar), Bernadette Rostenkowski-Wolowitz (Melissa Rauch), and Amy Farrah Fowler (Mayim Bialik)—bonded over science and pop culture.

The Big Bang Theory had astroparticle physicist David Saltzberg on retainer from the beginning of the series. He attended the tapings every week, offering corrections and ensuring the whiteboards used in the scenes were accurate. In season one episode "The Cooper-Hofstadter Polarization," Saltzberg even wrote a joke for Sheldon, who gets into an argument with Leonard. When Penny asks Sheldon about the "little misunderstanding," Sheldon replies, "A little misunderstanding? Galileo and the pope had a little misunderstanding!"

Even though Saltzberg is the chair of UCLA's Physics & Astronomy department and regularly publishes papers, he thinks his work on *The Big Bang Theory* has been even more impactful. "It's hard to fathom, when you think about twenty million viewers on the first showing—and that doesn't include other countries and reruns," Saltzberg told NPR. "I'm happy if a paper I write gets read by a dozen people."

Silicon Valley (2014–2019)

Mike Judge's obsessively detailed satire of life in the tech industry follows Richard Hendricks (Thomas Middleditch) as he attempts to build a start-up around a revolutionary algorithm he created in his spare time. Pied Piper's ragtag team of coding misfits have the technical skills to change the world, if only they could stop getting in each other's (and their own) way. Martin Starr (Bertram Gilfoyle), Kumail

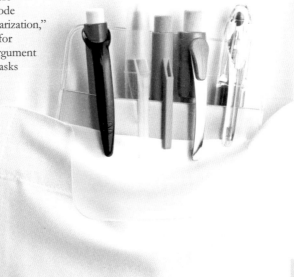

Nanjiani (Dinesh Chugtai), Zach Woods (Jared Dunn), and T. J. Miller (Erlich Bachman)—who left the show after its fourth of six seasons—co-star.

Judge, who had logged some hours as an engineer in the real Silicon Valley, first toyed around with the idea of a project centered on America's tech giants more than ten years before *Silicon Valley* made its debut in 2014. "Way back, before the dot-com burst in 2000, I thought about doing something like this, about a tech billionaire [Microsoft co-founder] Paul Allen–type, but that was as a movie," Judge told Deadline during the show's first season.

When discussing the authenticity of the series, Judge told *Esquire* that his past experience as an engineer working in Silicon Valley certainly helps, especially as "the personality types haven't changed that much." But executive producer and co-showrunner Alec Berg shared that the writers really immerse themselves in the research: "At the beginning of each season, the entire writing staff goes up to San Francisco and the Valley for about a

week. We pack our days with meetings with start-ups and with venture capitalists and different serial entrepreneurs. We have lunches and dinners with all kinds of oddball people with a lot of interesting thoughts."

 REPLAY

If you've ever wondered what Pied Piper's website might look like if the company at the center of *Silicon Valley* existed in real life, you're in luck: HBO built a website for the company, PiedPiper.com, complete with company bios, a blog (written by Jared), cheesy font, and banner that proudly touts the fact that, "Pied Piper's Space Saver App Hits Top 500 in Hooli App Store!"

MATCH THE THEME SONG TO ITS TV SERIES:

_____ I. "Superman"

_____ 2. "Where You Lead"

_____ 3. "The History of Everything"

_____ 4. "Boss of Me"

_____ 5. "Way Down in the Hole"

_____ 6. "Thank You for Being a Friend"

A. *The Big Bang Theory*

B. *The Golden Girls*

C. *Gilmore Girls*

D. *Scrubs*

E. *Malcolm in the Middle*

F. *The Wire*

RECASTING: THE BIG BANG THEORY

The Big Bang Theory is being rebooted and it's your chance to play the casting director. Who are you hiring to play each of the key roles?

Sheldon Cooper _____

Leonard Hofstadter _____

Penny Hofstadter _____

Howard Wolowitz _____

Bernadette Rostenkowski-Wolowitz _____

Raj Koothrappali _____

Amy Farrah Fowler _____

Stuart Bloom _____

Dr. Beverly Hofstadter _____

Priya Koothrappali _____

TECH SUPPORT

You don't need to know your IP address from your ISP to enjoy these tech-heavy dramas.

Black Mirror (2011–2019)

Warning: Do not attempt to binge-watch all of *Black Mirror* in a single day or weekend. There are only a few short seasons, so it might sound tempting—and yes, you could physically do it . . . but mentally, you're going to need a little breathing room.

Though the anthology series has been compared to *The Twilight Zone* due to its twisty, technology-themed tales, at its heart, *Black Mirror* is a reflection of society. "The technology is never the culprit in our stories," creator Charlie Brooker told *Vogue*. "The technology is just allowing people to do terrible things to themselves or others." It only takes watching the first episode to understand what Brooker is talking about.

Halt and Catch Fire (2014–2017)

Halt and Catch Fire is Christopher Cantwell and Christopher C. Rogers's 1980s-set throwback to the birth of the personal computer and the revolution (and competition) it inspired. Lee Pace stars as Joe MacMillan, a magnetic entrepreneur who has big ideas but no technical skills, which puts him at the mercy of people like Gordon Clark (Scoot McNairy) and Cameron Howe (Mackenzie Davis), the computer prodigies he tasks with reverse-engineering IBM's revolutionary PC so that he can catch up to the competition, then think one step ahead.

Halt and Catch Fire never got the audience it deserved when it was airing, which means many people don't know just how brilliant and daring the show was—particularly in the latter of its four seasons, which included a time jump, a shocking death, and the dawn of the internet age. Its finale in particular is one of its finest hours, as it's all about closing old chapters and starting new ones. It sends the show's trinity of remaining major characters in promising new directions, even as they all come to terms with the fact that they can never again recapture what they once had. And if you're wondering what that title means: It's an early computer command that would cause a computer's central processing unit (CPU) to cease meaningful operation.

MATCH THE TV SERIES THAT HAD BIZARRE CROSSOVERS WITH EACH OTHER:

____ 1. *Mr. Robot*   A. *Scooby-Doo*

____ 2. *The X-Files*   B. *Eastenders*

____ 3. *Supernatural*   C. *The Simpsons*

____ 4. *Doctor Who*   D. *Cops*

____ 5. *24*   E. *ALF*

Mr. Robot (2015–2019)

On June 24, 2015, USA Network premiered *Mr. Robot*, a New York City–based thriller-drama about Elliot Alderson (Rami Malek), an alienated and drug-addled vigilante hacker who uses his skills to hack into E Corp, one of the world's largest corporations, and erase all consumer debt. This financial shake-up is just one part of the mission of fsociety, a group of anarchist hackers who recruit Elliot to work with them, using their tech skills to change the world.

For four seasons, the acclaimed series—created by and mostly written and directed by Sam Esmail—explored isolation, hacker culture, blurred reality, cybersecurity, mental illness, family ties, and the deadly effects of capitalism.

Malek won an Emmy for his performance, and near the end of the show's run, he also won an Oscar for the Freddie Mercury biopic *Bohemian Rhapsody*. On December 22, 2019, *Mr. Robot* logged off for good.

During a showrunner roundtable discussion with *The Hollywood Reporter*, Esmail revealed that *Mr. Robot* was partially autobiographical. "Elliot is a thinly veiled version of myself," he said. "I wrote what I knew because a lot of the details of his life and the loneliness were issues I've dealt with basically my whole life."

What is the first TV series you remember binge-watching?

Which series better lend themselves to a straight binge-watch?

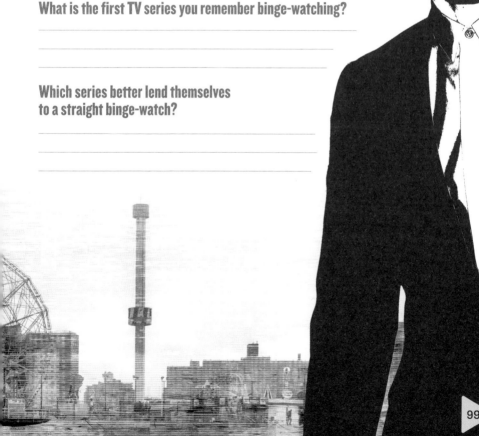

APOCALYPSE NOW

If your idea of escapism involves oppressive governments and zombie-infested civilizations, these dystopian TV shows should scratch your bleak-and-depressing itch.

The Walking Dead (2010–2022)

Zombies have always been a dependable crowd-pleaser, but *The Walking Dead* proves that tales of the living impaired can also spawn a multibillion dollar franchise complete with video games, toys, spin-offs, and all the other windfalls network executives dream of.

Based on the hit Image Comics series by writer Robert Kirkman and artists Tony Moore and Charlie Adlard, *The Walking Dead* already had an award-winning foundation when producer Frank Darabont first brought the adaptation to AMC. The show itself mirrors its comic book roots by following Rick Grimes (Andrew Lincoln) and a group of other survivors (Jon Bernthal, Sarah Wayne Callies, Norman Reedus, and more) who have to eke out an existence in a post-apocalyptic world overrun by the undead. Human nature being what it is, they soon find themselves at odds with one another and other factions of survivors, proving that the flesh-eaters might not be their biggest threat after all.

The Leftovers (2014–2017)

A one-sentence summary of HBO's *The Leftovers* might sound something like this: "Three years after 2 percent of the world's population has vanished without a trace, suburban sheriff Kevin Garvey (Justin Theroux) and other survivors cope with

MATCH *THE WALKING DEAD* CHARACTER WITH THEIR WEAPON OF CHOICE:

_____ 1. Rick Grimes   A. Main battle tank

_____ 2. Negan Smith   B. Katana

_____ 3. Daryl Dixon   C. Colt Python revolver

_____ 4. Michonne Hawthorne   D. Shotgun

_____ 5. The Governor   E. Knife hand

_____ 6. Merle Dixon   F. Crossbow

_____ 7. Shane Walsh   G. Baseball bat

the loss in different ways." In terms of comprehensiveness, that's a little like describing the *Bible*'s New Testament as "a story about how God's son was born on Earth, made some friends and enemies, was killed, and came back to life."

The Leftovers was based on Tom Perrotta's novel of the same name, which imagines the world after an ostensibly non-religious rapture known as the Sudden Departure. But co-creator Damon Lindelof (*Lost*) had covered all of Perrotta's published territory by the end of season one, which allowed him (with Perrotta's help) to expand the scope of the series in virtually every direction—first to a town untouched by the catastrophe, then to Australia—with increasingly frequent side quests into the subconscious and spiritual realms. Though its fan base was built slowly and quietly, *The Leftovers* is now regarded by many as one of the most innovative shows of all time—and one that assumes its viewers are smart enough to draw their own conclusions.

Though the Sudden Departure hangs like a pall over everything else in the series, its creators maintained from the get-go that the show was never going to be about why it happened or where the victims went. But they weren't exactly withholding much-coveted details from the audience; they simply never made up a backstory. When Lindelof first met with Perrotta about partnering on a TV adaptation, he asked the author if he at least knew what had happened to everyone. As Lindelof told *Variety*, "[Perrotta] said in the most kind and generous and authentically honest way: 'I got to be honest with you, man, I've never even thought about it.'"

The Handmaid's Tale (2017–present)

Though Hulu had been producing original content for years, it wasn't until 2017—and the debut of *The Handmaid's Tale*—that audiences really started to pay attention. The dystopian drama, based on Margaret Atwood's 1985 book, imagines a future in which a theocratic regime known as Gilead has taken over the United States and enslaved fertile women so that the group's most powerful couples can procreate. (Infertile women who aren't wives are typically cooks and housekeepers known as Marthas.)

If it all sounds rather bleak, that's because it is. So if you're looking for a sunny pick-me-up, *The Handmaid's Tale* is not it. And while its story is an exaggeration of any male-dominated society that currently exists, there are many truths hidden within the series that speak to the realities of today. Elisabeth Moss stars as Offred, a fertile woman in an infertile land who is bound (practically literally) to a military officer (Joseph Fiennes) in Gilead's middle management. As a handmaid, it's Offred's job to bear children for this officer and his wife, but Offred (real name June Osborne) isn't big on being told what to do. Which is where the real story begins.

Reed Morano, who created the look of the show while directing its first three episodes, felt a certain political responsibility while working on the show. She was astonished to learn how many people don't vote or recognize that their voice matters. "We're too complacent," Morano told *Esquire*. "We let things happen to us. And you don't have to let things happen to you. You can effect change."

SHOWS THAT WERE AHEAD OF THEIR TIME

SHOW: _____

WHY: _____

SHOW: _____

WHY: _____

SHOW: _____

WHY: _____

SHOW: _____

WHY: _____

SHOW: _____

WHY: _____

SHOW: _____

WHY: _____

SHOW: _____

WHY: _____

SHOW: _____

WHY: _____

SHOW: _____

WHY: _____

SHOW: _____

WHY: _____

SHOW: _____

WHY: _____

SHOW: _____

WHY: _____

SHOW: _____

WHY: _____

SHOW: _____

WHY: _____

SHOW: _____

WHY: _____

SHOW: _____

WHY: _____

SHOW: _____

WHY: _____

SHOW: _____

WHY: _____

SHOW: _____

WHY: _____

SHOW: _____

WHY: _____

WORLDS BEYOND

From political intrigue on an intergalactic scale to an old-fashioned space Western done right, the sci-fi genre has no shortage of bingeable hits.

Battlestar Galactica (2004–2009)

In the early 2000s, producer David Eick and writer Ronald D. Moore began working on a reboot of *Battlestar Galactica*, the 1978 sci-fi TV series that most people seemed to have forgotten all about. It follows the adventures of a human battleship in deep space attempting to avoid the Cylons, a race of AI beings intent on destroying the

fifty-thousand humans left in the world. By tapping into some of their own past storytelling frustrations, as well as the fears and concerns of post-9/11 America, Eick and Moore began constructing what would become one of the most acclaimed television series of the twenty-first century.

The road to *Battlestar Galactica* becoming a giant of 2000s television was not an easy one, though. Its creators fought through a fandom that hated the very idea of a reboot and a supposed "plan" that didn't really exist, all to establish a new vision of sci-fi television with an all-star cast that included Oscar nominees Edward James Olmos (William Adama) and Mary McDonnell (Laura Roslin)—and Katee Sackhoff in the role of Starbuck, which caused some unexpected controversy.

Moore wanted to make his intentions for *Battlestar Galactica*—which began as a miniseries for Syfy before the channel ultimately greenlit it as an ongoing series— clear from the beginning. To do this, he included a three-page manifesto of sorts at the beginning of the miniseries script,

a document that has now become legendary to fans. Titled "Naturalistic Science Fiction, or Taking the Opera out of Space Opera," Moore began the document with a simple but grand mission statement: "Our goal is nothing less than the reinvention of the science fiction television series."

The document remained attached to the script as it went out to actors, and the philosophy drew some of the show's most important stars, including Olmos, to the series.

Star Trek: Discovery (2017–present)

Set before the events of the original *Star Trek* series (with suspiciously sleeker costumes and tech), *Star Trek: Discovery* kicks off with an accidental war between the United Federation of Planets and the Klingon Empire, caused by the insubordination of Commander Michael Burnham (Sonequa Martin-Green). She's reassigned to starship *Discovery*, which can move to any point in space instantaneously by using an experimental spore drive (yes, it runs on mushrooms). The show includes some of the classic *Star Trek* "planet of the week" vibes, but it deals far more with bold, season-long plots as well as the intimate lives of its crew.

Discovery is also the first *Star Trek* series to feature openly gay characters: Astromycologist Paul Stamets (Anthony Rapp) and his husband, medical officer Hugh Culber (Wilson Cruz).

The Mandalorian (2020–present)

In the ever-expanding *Star Wars* universe, *The Mandolorian*—which takes place five years after the downfall of the Empire in *Return of the Jedi*—features Pedro Pascal as an armored bounty hunter who's a lot more like The Man with No Name than Buck Rogers. Jaded and exhausted by his profession and the dwindling hopes for his oppressed compatriots, Mando picks up a dangerous gig transporting precious cargo in the form of Baby Yoda (a.k.a. The Child; a.k.a. Grogu) and decides to protect the fifty-year-old child instead of collecting the bounty. Now, the entire universe is on their tail.

While the *Star Wars* universe has long been on the bleeding edge of cinematic technology, series creator Jon Favreau has opted to use old-school techniques whenever possible. Case in point: Grogu, the show's breakout star, is not a CGI creation—he's an actual puppet, and an expensive one at that. Favreau has put his cost at about $5 million.

MANY SPACE SHOWS, INCLUDING STAR TREK: DISCOVERY AND BATTLESTAR GALACTICA, ARE NAMED AFTER THEIR SHIPS. MATCH THE FOLLOWING SHOWS WITH THE MAIN SHIP'S NAME:

____ 1. *Star Trek*   A. *Moya*

____ 2. *Firefly*   B. *Daedalus*

____ 3. *Farscape*   C. *Razor Crest*

____ 4. *The Mandalorian*   D. USS *Enterprise*

____ 5. *Stargate SG-1*   E. *Serenity*

Which retro TV show do you think is ripe for a reboot?

WHY:

_____

_____

_____

Fantastic Voyages

Suspension of disbelief is the only requirement for enjoying these series, which take us to places and worlds real and imagined.

Doctor Who (1963–1989; 2005–present)

Doctor Who is the kind of sci-fi juggernaut that can seem a bit daunting to anyone who isn't a hardcore fan of the genre. While the original incarnation has a definite sense of humor, the reimagined version of the series—which made its triumphant return in 2005—offers loads of kitschy fun. The series follows an alien known as the Doctor (no, it's *not* Doctor Who) who travels through space and time in a vehicle known as the TARDIS, which is disguised as a British police call box, to help save the world with the help of his trusty (and ever-changing) companions.

Though the reboot kicked off with Christopher Eccleston playing the Ninth Doctor, part of the fun of the series is that regeneration is canon—so while the Doctor is technically always the same character, he (or she) can regenerate into a new face and body every time an actor leaves the show. David Tennant, Matt Smith, and Peter Capaldi followed Eccleston, and in 2017, viewers got their first glimpse of *Broadchurch* star Jodie Whittaker—the first woman to take on the role of the Doctor—in the Christmas special "Twice Upon a Time."

These regenerations were introduced when William Hartnell, who played the First Doctor from 1963 to 1966, faced health issues that forced him to leave the series. To ensure that the show could go on without its original star, and to avoid enraging viewers who adored Hartnell, the showrunners decided that the ability to regenerate would become a part of the Doctor's mythology. Years after it was written, an internal BBC memo was uncovered that outlined the "metaphysical change" that would take place as the First Doctor became the Second Doctor (Patrick Troughton). "It is as if he had had the LSD drug, and instead of experiencing the kicks, he has the hell and dank horror which can be its effect," the memo explained.

Lost (2004–2010)

On the surface, *Lost* might seem to be a typical adventure show featuring survivors of a plane crash who are stranded on a tropical island and must learn how to work together in order to survive. But the show doesn't take long to reveal its strange side—and the less you know about that going in, the better. Let's just say the island has many secrets . . . though not nearly as many as the survivors themselves, whose pre-crash backstories are doled out in flashbacks. *Lost's* many mysteries compelled viewers to

SURVIVOR OR OTHER?

IS EACH OF THESE *LOST* CHARACTERS AN OCEANIC FLIGHT 815 SURVIVOR, OR ONE OF "THE OTHERS"?

_____ I. John Locke

_____ 2. Nikki Fernandez

_____ 3. Jacob

_____ 4. Ben Linus

_____ 5. Shannon Rutherford

_____ 6. Juliet Burke

_____ 7. Charlie Pace

_____ 8. Michael Dawson

_____ 9. Alexandra Rousseau

_____ I0. Danny Pickett

try to figure out what was happening, searching for clues, analyzing the science, and theorizing on social media as few fan bases had ever done before.

Speaking with *Grantland*, showrunner Carlton Cuse compared the first season of *Lost* to "putting out an apartment fire with a garden hose. We had some general ideas of what we were going to do, but we were making the show episode to episode." *Lost* co-creator and co-showrunner Damon Lindelof used a rolling method for establishing the "truths" behind various island mysteries, intending to slowly provide answers over time but leaving the unrevealed answers open for competition. A healthy rivalry developed with writers trying to dethrone the accepted wisdom.

When it came time to end *Lost*, the producers made the conscious decision not to try to answer every lingering question. Instead, recognizing that nothing they did would satisfy every single fan, Lindelof told *The Independent* that "we wanted to try

to answer a mystery the show hadn't even asked up until that point . . . what happens when you die and the process that you go through in order to achieve some fundamental level of grace."

Its divisive ending has led to many debates about the show's legacy, but as *Entertainment Weekly*'s Jeff Lenson wrote, "What is certain is that *Lost* helped change the way we watch and talk about television."

Supernatural (2005–2020)

Prepare your mind, body, and favorite screen for the potential long-term investment that is bingeing all 327 episodes of *Supernatural*. The fantasy drama follows charismatic, monster-hunting brothers Dean (Jensen Ackles) and Sam Winchester (Jared Padalecki) as they travel the country looking for otherworldly baddies, spurred by their father's (Jeffrey Dean Morgan) disappearance and the death of their mother (Samantha Smith). If it turns out to be your cup of tea, also be prepared to join the legion of fans who, having invested so much time in the labyrinthine world-building done over the course of the show's full run, see *Supernatural* as less of a TV series and more of a cult-like religious experience.

Amazingly, pretty much no one involved with *Supernatural* expected it to last as long as it did. Creator Eric Kripke even titled the season five finale "Swan Song," as he expected it to be their final episode, never guessing it would run for another ten seasons.

Who's the actor you'd most love to see play The Doctor on *Doctor Who*?

_____

WHY:

IT'S A SCREAM

Settle in for a monster of a binge-watching marathon with these shows that pack both thrills and chills.

American Horror Story (2011–present)

American Horror Story is a lot of creepy shows collected together under one banner. Created by *Glee* colleagues Ryan Murphy and Brad Falchuk, each season explores a new horrifying milieu, from the ghosts of its Los Angeles murder house to the witches of its New Orleans coven to the stabby sleepaway camp of its *1984* entry. The show has a repertory cast, so even though the freakish characters change with each haunt, the familiar faces of Sarah Paulson, Emma Roberts, Lily Rabe, Evan Peters, and more are there to make us feel comfortably unsettled.

While exploring nearly a dozen classic horror concepts, the show has made it a point to include real-life events in its abattoir: Serial killer John Wayne Gacy offers inspiration for several plots, *Coven* cast Kathy Bates as the murderous nineteenth-century socialite Madame Delphine LaLaurie, and the hotel-set fifth season takes its cues from several bloody tales from the infamous Cecil Hotel—a reportedly haunted Los Angeles hotel and apartment building that has been investigated by Zak Bagans and the *Ghost*

WHICH SOMETIMES TERRIFYING ANTHOLOGY SERIES FEATURED AN EPISODE TITLED "ALL THROUGH THE HOUSE," IN WHICH AN ESCAPED MANIAC DRESSED UP LIKE SANTA TERRORIZES A WOMAN IN HER OWN HOME?

_____ A. *Creepshow*

_____ B. *American Horror Story*

_____ C. *The Twilight Zone*

_____ D. *Tales from the Crypt*

Adventures crew and was the subject of the 2021 Netflix true crime docuseries *Crime Scene: The Vanishing at the Cecil Hotel.*

Penny Dreadful (2014–2016)

Penny Dreadful features a murderer's row of gothic literary horror figures: Dorian Gray (Reeve Carney), Dr. Victor Frankenstein (Harry Treadaway), Frankenstein's monster (Rory Kinnear), and even the Bride of Frankenstein (Billie Piper) play prominent roles, with Count Dracula (Christian Camargo), Van Helsing (David Warner), Renfield (Samuel Barnett), and more getting involved in the spooky fun. Eva Green stars as Vanessa Ives, a mysterious figure who, alongside adventurer Malcolm Murray (Timothy Dalton), hires the American sideshow gunman Ethan Chandler (Josh Hartnett) to find Murray's daughter.

This is just the starting point for a sprawling quest that involves rebuking romantic advances from Lucifer and making living people out of dead parts. The show's title, of course, is a reference to the fantastically cheap, gratuitous genre story rags offered in nineteenth-century England, and the show's tone reflects the grounded, gruesome sensibility that came with those stories, which were meant to shock.

But just as quickly as it appeared, this gorgeously shot and designed series ended after twenty-seven episodes, with many fans only realizing that the show was officially coming to an end when the words "The End" actually appeared on the screen.

In 2020, a spin-off series, *Penny Dreadful: City of Angels*, premiered on Showtime, though its connection was merely a spiritual one. It was canceled after one season.

Who's a famous horror villain you'd like to see get the TV treatment?

Stranger Things creators Matt and Ross Duffer and casting director Carmen Cuba auditioned 1,213 child actors to get the right mix of kids for what would be crucial roles in the series. When you're going up against that kind of competition, it helps to have someone influential in your corner—and Millie Bobby Brown had a horror heavyweight. Stephen King saw Brown in the BBC show *Intruders* and publicly praised her work on Twitter, calling her "terrific" and asking, "Is it my imagination, or are child actors a lot better than they used to be?" thus giving her a leg up in the race to become a stranger thing.

Stranger Things (2016–present)

The kids and monsters of *Stranger Things* own our Steven Spielberg–loving hearts. Set in the tiny town of Hawkins, Indiana, in the 1980s, the hit Netflix series is packed with retro homages and meta-references to the pop culture of the era—from *Dungeons & Dragons* to Stephen King. The series follows a group of kids, including the mysterious and psychokinetic Eleven (Millie Bobby Brown), as they navigate adolescence in a dangerous world filled with face-splitting beasts from an alternate dimension known as the Upside Down and phones that do not work unless they're tethered to the wall. *Terrifying!*

There aren't any transdimensional horror-beasts rampaging through quiet suburban towns (that we know of), but *Stranger Things* is based on real conspiracy theories about the American government conducting reality-bending experiments on children—specifically, the Montauk Project, which has been referenced in other works of fiction, such as Thomas Pynchon's novel *Bleeding Edge*. Much of what Eleven experiences in the laboratory corresponds to the alleged activities of the Montauk Project. The show was also initially called *Montauk* and set on the far end of the Long Island peninsula.

SHOW: _____   WHY: _____
_____

SHOW: _____   WHY: _____
_____

SHOW: _____   WHY: _____
_____

SHOW: _____   WHY: _____
_____

SHOW: _____   WHY: _____
_____

SHOW: _____   WHY: _____
_____

SHOW: _____   WHY: _____
_____

SHOW: _____   WHY: _____
_____

SHOW: _____   WHY: _____
_____

SHOW: _____   WHY: _____
_____

MUSIC, MAN

Musicals are a tough needle to thread, but when the elements are just right—great music, talented performers, and tunes that help push a TV show's narrative forward—actors breaking into song can actually be pretty enthralling.

Empire (2015–2020)
Family alliances are forged and betrayed against a backdrop of chart-worthy original R & B songs as Lucious Lyon (Terrence Howard) decides which son should inherit his record label. His wife Cookie's (Taraji P. Henson) recent release from prison complicates the process but makes the series especially entertaining.

Flight of The Conchords (2007–2009)
Jemaine Clement and Bret McKenzie are Flight of the Conchords—a band that used to be "New Zealand's fourth most popular guitar-based digi-bongo acapella-rap-funk-comedy folk duo" but are now "the almost award-winning fourth-most-popular folk duo in New Zealand." They're also the stars of this delightfully absurd comedy where the slightest observation or most mundane conversation can turn into a surprisingly catchy tune like "Too Many Dicks (on the Dance Floor)."

Nashville (2012–2018)
Aging country music queen Rayna Jaymes (Connie Britton) fights tooth and perfectly-lacquered nail to keep a sought-after new singer (Hayden Panettiere) from eclipsing her stardom. Nashville is both a fascinating look at the country music scene and a CMT music video come to life.

Smash (2012–2013)
For the casual viewer, Smash is a drama about a bunch of triple threats jockeying for roles in new Broadway musicals. For musical theater buffs, it's more about recognizing the many familiar Broadway faces who appear in the show: Christian Borle, Annaleigh Ashford, and Leslie Odom Jr., to name a few.

MATCH THE MUSICIAN TO THE SHOW ON WHICH THEY MADE A CAMEO:

____ 1. Katy Perry   A. *Game of Thrones*

____ 2. Cher   B. *Ugly Betty*

____ 3. David Bowie   C. *Glee*

____ 4. Eve   D. *How I Met Your Mother*

____ 5. Adele   E. *Will & Grace*

____ 6. Ed Sheeran   F. *Extras*

MY FAVORITE SHOWS OF ALL TIME

SHOW: _____ WHY: _____

_____

SHOW: _____ WHY: _____

_____

SHOW: _____ WHY: _____

_____

SHOW: _____ WHY: _____

_____

SHOW: _____ WHY: _____

_____

SHOW: _____ WHY: _____

_____

SHOW: _____ WHY: _____

_____

SHOW: _____ WHY: _____

_____

SHOW: _____ WHY: _____

_____

SHOW: _____ WHY: _____

_____

RAP IT UP

The rap scene might be the shared backdrop of these series, but where the artists take it from there is part of each show's own unique journey.

The Get Down (2016–2017)

Oscar nominee Baz Luhrmann (*Moulin Rouge*) and Pulitzer Prize winner Stephen Adly Guirgis co-created this short-lived series for Netflix. Set in the Bronx in the 1970s, *The Get Down* explored the rise of rap, hip-hop, and disco music through the perspective of a group of teenagers. Led by then-largely-unknown actors like Justice Smith (Ezekiel "Books" Figuero), Shameik Moore (Shaolin Fantastic), Herizen Guardiola (Mylene Cruz), and Yahya Abdul-Mateen (Cadillac), the show featured supporting turns from Jaden Smith (Marcus "Dizzee" Kipling), Daveed Diggs (adult Ezekiel "Mr. Books" Figuero), Giancarlo Esposito (Pastor Ramon Cruz), and Jimmy Smits (Francisco "Papa Fuerte" Cruz), who personified the generational differences that came into sharp focus with the advent of this urgent new indigenous art form.

Luhrmann's kitchen-sink storytelling approach may not always have been the best choice for exploring the quieter inner lives of this community, much less its complex history, but he was nevertheless provided with incredible financial resources to do so: At a cost of $10 million per episode, the show formed a three-way-tie with *Friends* and *Game of Thrones* for the then-highest budget per episode in television history.

Atlanta (2016–present)

It didn't take long for Donald Glover's *Atlanta*—a show about fame and friendship—to start burning down screens by subverting expectations for what a TV series can be. The show sets

REPLAY

Before Donald Glover starred on *Community*, made it big as rapper Childish Gambino, or created *Atlanta*, he was a writer on *30 Rock*. "He was actually still . . . living in an NYU dorm. He was an RA," Tina Fey told *Entertainment Weekly*. He also wrote some of the lyrics to *30 Rock*'s iconic song "Werewolf Bar Mitzvah."

MATCH THE SONG TITLE TO THE ACTOR WHO RELEASED IT:

_____ 1. "Party All the Time" A. Eddie Murphy

_____ 2. "How Do I Deal" B. Joey Lawrence

_____ 3. "Respect Yourself" C. Leonard Nimoy

_____ 4. "Nothing My Love Can't Fix" D. Jennifer Love Hewitt

_____ 5. "The Ballad of Bilbo Baggins" E. Bruce Willis

up a classic narrative: Rapper Paper Boi (Brian Tyree Henry) is making a name for himself as he rises from underground to commercial success in the rap world, with his cousin and manager Earnest, a.k.a. Earn (Glover), at his side. Then the show pushes that deep into the background in favor of heavy atmosphere and fraught character relationships.

The principal cast, including Glover, Henry, LaKeith Stanfield, and Zazie Beetz, anchors the show with some of the most charismatic and human performances on television. *Atlanta*, which is equal parts funny, frightening, entrancing, and enlightening, revels in a freedom few shows ever attain—and it does so in nearly every episode. Trippy and grounded, silly and brutal, *Atlanta* defies a singular label and demands a seat at the VIP table.

Along with surrealism, *Atlanta* trades in the kind of wry humor that would make Larry David proud, which explains why Glover describes the show as a rapper version of *Curb Your Enthusiasm.* "Being a rapper is super awkward," Glover told Stephen Colbert in 2018. "You're in a video and you got, like, champagne and butts close to your face . . .

and then you have to go to Whole Foods and the person is like, 'Hey, you're that dude!' and you're like, 'Please, I really want to buy this ice cream.'" Cue the theme music and deadpan stare.

Dave (2020–present)

If you're wondering if a sitcom should exist to explore the career of a white rapper making his way in a musical milieu created by Black artists, rest assured that this sitcom is wondering that aloud the whole time.

Dave focuses on the exploits of Dave Burd, better known as comedically oriented rapper Lil Dicky. Not only does *Dave* feature some of the best characters on TV, but it actively wrestles with the identities of those characters and the way characters like them are used as tropes in storytelling and culture while delivering some of the smartest and most inventive storytelling around.

Skip to season one's fifth episode, "Hype Man," for one of the most illuminating and thoughtful portraits of bipolar disorder seen on television, then scroll back to the beginning to watch this extremely talented rapper reckon with his rights, and his role, in contemporary hip-hop.

Two Degrees of...
Donald Glover

Fill in the title of the TV show or movie that connects these actors to *Atlanta* star Donald Glover.

TIMOTHY OLYPHANT
was in

_____
TV SHOW OR MOVIE NAME
(2014) with Connie Britton, who was in

_____
TV SHOW OR MOVIE NAME
(2013) with Donald Glover.

UZO ADUBA
was in

_____
TV SHOW OR MOVIE NAME
(2017) with Emily Blunt, who was in

_____
TV SHOW OR MOVIE NAME
(2011) with Donald Glover.

CHARLES DANCE
was in

_____
TV SHOW OR MOVIE NAME
(2016) with Kristen Wiig, who was in

_____
TV SHOW OR MOVIE NAME
(2015) with Donald Glover.

MICHAEL SHANNON
was in

TV SHOW OR MOVIE NAME
(2011) with Jessica Chastain, who was in

TV SHOW OR MOVIE NAME
(2015) with Donald Glover.

BRUCE WILLIS
was in

TV SHOW OR MOVIE NAME
(1997) with Jack Black, who was in

TV SHOW OR MOVIE NAME
(2011) with Donald Glover.

SARAH PAULSON
was in

TV SHOW OR MOVIE NAME
(2016) with Mark Duplass, who was in

TV SHOW OR MOVIE NAME
(2015) with Donald Glover.

SHOWS I WANT TO WATCH

- [ ] _____
- [ ] _____
- [ ] _____
- [ ] _____
- [ ] _____
- [ ] _____
- [ ] _____
- [ ] _____
- [ ] _____
- [ ] _____
- [ ] _____
- [ ] _____
- [ ] _____
- [ ] _____
- [ ] _____

- [ ] _____
- [ ] _____
- [ ] _____
- [ ] _____
- [ ] _____
- [ ] _____
- [ ] _____
- [ ] _____
- [ ] _____
- [ ] _____
- [ ] _____
- [ ] _____
- [ ] _____
- [ ] _____
- [ ] _____

MEDICAL ATTENTION

Life and death consequences make for some of television's most compelling—and long-running—series.

ER (1994–2009)

Novelist Michael Crichton, who was a student at Harvard Medical School in the 1960s, wrote a movie screenplay about his time there, which executive producer John Wells used as the basis of the series *ER*, set at Chicago's fictional County General Hospital. During its fifteen-year run, the show cycled through a number of amazing actors, but few could compete with George Clooney, who played pediatrician Doug Ross.

"Clooney begged me for a part," Wells later said. A TV veteran at thirty-three years old, Clooney was ready for his breakout role: "George was the first person to audition. He came after me for it," Wells recalled.

MATCH THE MEDICAL DRAMA TO ITS HOSPITAL:

____ 1. *Scrubs*

____ 2. *ER*

____ 3. *Grey's Anatomy*

____ 4. *House*

____ 5. *Nurse Jackie*

A. Seattle Grace Hospital

B. All Saints' Hospital

C. Princeton-Plainsboro Teaching Hospital

D. County General Hospital

E. Sacred Heart Hospital

Scrubs (2001–2010)

Scrubs follows the surreal daydreams of John "J. D." Dorian (Zach Braff) and his fellow medical interns as they train to become doctors. "One of the things I swore to the female actors on the show was 'You guys will have to be in skimpy lingerie and doing sexy shit, but I promise you for every time one of you guys is like that one of the male characters will be like that,'" creator Bill Lawrence later said. That certainly explains The Todd's frequent appearances in a banana hammock.

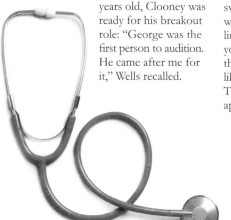

Grey's Anatomy (2005–present)

Shonda Rhimes told Oprah Winfrey that although she had always loved shows about surgery and emergency rooms, the unique angle for her show was sparked after a doctor mentioned how hard it was to shave her legs in the hospital shower. "At first that seemed like a silly detail," Rhimes said. "But then I thought about the fact that it was the only time and place this woman might have to shave her legs. That's how hard the work is."

While the core cast of *Grey's* has changed over the seasons, Patrick Dempsey's character, Dr. Derek Shepherd, has remained a favorite of both fans and the show's creators. "When we were shooting the pilot, Patrick was seriously the most adorable man we'd ever seen on camera," Rhimes told Oprah. "We'd watch the monitor and think, 'Look at his dreamy eyes!' So we started calling him Patrick McDreamy, and it stuck."

3 Skills I Learned from TV

1 _____

2 _____

3 _____

1

ER

Noah Wyle, who played Dr. John Carter on *ER*, was shooting an episode of *ER* in Africa's Kalahari Desert when the on-set medic passed out from the heat. Wyle took a functioning IV, stuck a needle in the medic, and revived him with a bag of saline, which he learned how to do from playing the role for so long (he filmed a total of 254 episodes of the series).

2

Grey's Anatomy

In 2011, when a Wisconsin woman collapsed during a severe asthma attack, her ten-year-old daughter and a friend administered CPR after seeing it done on *Grey's Anatomy*. The woman made a full recovery.

4 TIMES TV SAVED SOMEONE'S LIFE

3

The Walking Dead

A California woman used skills she learned from *The Walking Dead* to defend herself from an attacker who was trying to stab her to death. She adopted the "kill or be killed" attitude from the show and successfully fought him off.

4

The Office

In *The Office*'s season five episode "Stress Relief," Michael Scott (Steve Carell) arranges a CPR training session for his staff that said that the chest compressions should be done to the beat of the popular Bee Gees song "Stayin' Alive." This tip helped an *Office* fan from Arizona successfully perform CPR on a woman he found slumped over in the seat of her car. She regained consciousness after about a minute of CPR and was brought to the hospital, where she recovered and was later discharged.

FILM FESTIVAL

Shows spun off from movies can seem like a crass commercial cash grab, but some series defy expectations and wind up looming larger in pop culture than their big-screen counterparts.

Fargo (2014–present)

Making the leap from movie to television show has rarely turned out to be a great idea (see the small-screen versions of *Ferris Bueller*, *Dirty Dancing*, and *Casablanca*). But *Fargo* is an exception to this rule. Brilliantly crafted, the show is technically designed as an anthology series, though there are small connections between each of its seasons.

Even better: The series doesn't try to retell the Coen brothers' Oscar-winning 1996 film, but it does pay tribute to their work—not

Cobra Kai (2018–present)

Picking up nearly thirty years after Daniel LaRusso (Ralph Macchio) was last seen on-screen in 1989's *The Karate Kid Part III*, the Netflix streaming series *Cobra Kai* has managed to bridge the gap between fans of the original film series that began with 1984's *The Karate Kid* and newcomers to the franchise who can follow a new crop of martial arts–obsessed teenagers.

In the show, LaRusso, winner of the 1984 All-Valley Karate Tournament, is now a successful car dealer. His high school rival, Johnny Lawrence (William Zabka), is a down-on-his-luck handyman who decides to look to his old dojo's principles for salvation. Naturally, their paths cross once again.

When *Cobra Kai* was conceived by producers Josh Heald, Jon Hurwitz, and Hayden Schlossberg, Macchio thought it was the right time to say yes to a *Karate Kid* revival after nearly three decades of turning offers down. "Listen, I've heard many, many pitches over thirty-plus years of why we wanna revisit this world, and it never seemed fresh," Macchio told Uproxx in 2020. "It was always easier to say no and protect the legacy because I'm very protective of it, and it was never smart enough." In a separate interview with Collider, Macchio said that many of the pitches involved LaRusso having a child who would prompt him to mirror the influence Mr. Miyagi (the late Pat Morita) had on LaRusso in the original films, but they had no substance beyond that. Seeing the universe through the eyes of Johnny Lawrence convinced Macchio the idea had merit.

Other Movies Turned TV Shows Worth a Watch

Ash vs. Evil Dead (2015–2018)

Bates Motel (2013–2017)

The Dark Crystal: Age of Resistance (2019)

Dear White People (2017–2021)

Four Weddings and a Funeral (2019)

Hanna (2019–2021)

Highlander: The Series (1992–1998)

She's Gotta Have It (2017–2019)

Tremors (2003)

Wet Hot American Summer (2015–2017)

just with its title or setting, but with its unique tone, quirky characters, and perfectly honed black comedy. Each season so far has taken a good guys versus bad guys approach, typically pitting the police against a handful of criminals, with a bumbling one usually thrown in for good measure.

Fargo series creator Noah Hawley had no desire to revisit Frances McDormand's Marge Gunderson character, the pregnant sheriff of Brainerd, Minnesota. Instead, as he told IndieWire in 2014, he wants to tell new stories each season and imagines that one day "people who see the movie might say, 'That was a really great episode of *Fargo*,' because each season is a separate true crime story from that region, the movie now fits into the series."

Because MGM owns the rights to *Fargo*, they didn't need the Coens' blessing to move forward. But when executive producer Warren Littlefield presented them with Hawley's script for the pilot, they decided to get involved. "They just said, 'We're not big fans of imitation, but we feel like Noah channeled us and we would like to put our names on this,'" Littlefield told HitFix in 2014. "And they didn't have to do that."

12 Monkeys (2015–2018)

The Syfy series *12 Monkeys* sent characters James Cole (Aaron Stanford), Dr. Cassandra Railly (Amanda Schull), Jennifer Goines (Emily Hampshire), José Ramse (Kirk Acevedo), Teddy Deacon (Todd Stashwick), and Dr. Katarina Jones (Barbara Sukowa) through basically every era of time you can imagine as they tried to save the world from the Army of the 12 Monkeys.

The TV version of the movie *12 Monkeys* began as a writing exercise for co-creator and showrunner Terry Matalas. "I'd always wanted to do a serialized time travel show," he told Mental Floss. "So I sat down at my kitchen table and started writing this thing called *Splinter*." After penning the first three acts, he handed the script off to his writing partner (and eventual co-creator) Travis Fickett, who wrote the back part of what would become *Splinter*'s pilot episode. The reactions to the sample were enthusiastic, and eventually, it ended up in the offices of Atlas, the production company that made Terry Gilliam's film version of *12 Monkeys*.

Atlas told Matalas and Fickett they'd been trying to turn the movie into a show for years and thought they could do it by reworking the *Splinter* spec script. Matalas suggested that, rather than rewriting the pilot entirely, they change some of the characters' names—"it was always about a woman named Cassie who was a virologist, but his name wasn't Cole, I think it was Max," Matalas said—and mention the Army of the 12 Monkeys at the very end of the episode, then go from there. "That just seemed like a really exciting way to reboot," Matalas said. "Having the intellectual property gave us an opportunity to expand that world [from the film], but at the same time, we could write it in the tone of what *Splinter* was. And so the rest is history."

Food for Thought

You'll want to fill up before digging into these reality series for foodies.

Top Chef (2006–present)

Today, reality TV–loving foodies are all too familiar with phrases like "Hands up, utensils down." But that wasn't the case until March 8, 2006, when Bravo's *Top Chef* first made its debut. In the nearly twenty years since, it's turned dozens of working chefs into household names and restaurant owners, including Stephanie Izard, who earned the James Beard Award for Best Chef in 2013, and the brothers Michael and Bryan Voltaggio. And the show's hosts have become celebrities in their own right.

Though it's impossible to talk about *Top Chef* without mentioning longtime host Padma Lakshmi, it's also easy to forget that she hasn't always been a part of the reality competition's winning formula. In season one, *Top Chef* was hosted by Katie Lee, a chef, food critic, and cookbook author. Bravo's Andy Cohen praised Lee in his official announcement of her departure from the series, calling her "a dynamic, beautiful woman who is passionate about food with a real zest for life."

Lakshmi joined the *Top Chef* hosts Tom Colicchio and Gail Simmons in the second season. While Food Network viewers were familiar with Lakshmi from her 2001 series, *Padma's Passport*, she also logged some time as an actress, most notably playing Sylk in Vondie Curtis-Hall's guilty pleasure *Glitter* (2001).

Chopped (2007–present)

One of Food Network's longest-running and most popular shows, *Chopped* pits four chefs against one another in a real-time competition for $10,000. There are three rounds per episode, typically broken down by "appetizer," "entrée," and "dessert." The chefs must bring their creativity and expertise in order to make use of every element included in the secret basket ingredients provided to them by the producers, which often seem at odds with one another, flavor-wise. A panel of three expert judges from the culinary community tastes their food and evaluates it based on taste, creativity, and presentation.

Over the show's approximately fifty seasons (they run a couple a year), the only true constant is change itself—in the unpredictable variety of ingredients and the development (or invention) of unique themes. But new contestants have learned some important lessons from their forebears to gain a potential edge: Be careful not to over-churn your ice cream during the dessert round, a deep fryer covers any number of mistakes, don't put hot liquid into a blender, and never, ever, ever try to make risotto in twenty minutes.

The Great British Baking Show (2010–present)

If you're an American fan of *The Great British Bake Off*, you probably know it better as *The Great British Baking Show* (though its most devoted fans, no matter where they live, simply call it GBBO, which saves a lot of time). A bona fide global sensation, the baking competition has the power to cause otherwise rational human beings to immediately run to their nearest supermarket in search of obscure ingredients like psyllium or Amarula cream liqueur. It's a charming, retro, warming hug of a TV show.

If you've ever wondered why the series is called *The Great British Bake Off* in England and *The Great British Baking Show* in America, the answer is simple: Pillsbury. The Pillsbury Bake Off, which began in 1949, is probably America's most famous baking contest, and the Pillsbury company owns the trademark to the phrase. So when

The Great British Bake Off crossed the pond, it became *The Great British Baking Show*.

It's difficult enough to make a cake that Paul Hollywood won't declare either under- or overbaked without having to worry about whether your oven is working properly. So for every day of filming, every oven has to be tested. And because this is a baking show, they're tested with cakes. Yes, every day, every oven has a Victoria sponge cake cooked in it to make sure everything's working exactly as it should.

4 FICTIONAL TV CHARACTERS I WOULD INVITE TO DINNER

1
WHY:

3
WHY:

2
WHY:

4
WHY:

SHOWS I WANT TO WATCH AGAIN

- [ ] _____
- [ ] _____
- [ ] _____
- [ ] _____
- [ ] _____
- [ ] _____
- [ ] _____
- [ ] _____
- [ ] _____
- [ ] _____
- [ ] _____
- [ ] _____
- [ ] _____

- [ ] _____
- [ ] _____
- [ ] _____
- [ ] _____
- [ ] _____
- [ ] _____
- [ ] _____
- [ ] _____
- [ ] _____
- [ ] _____
- [ ] _____
- [ ] _____

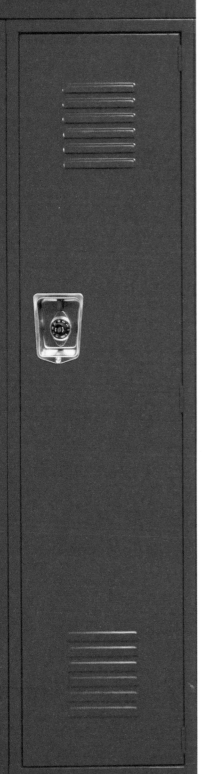

High school is a stressful time for even the most well-adjusted teen—unless you're viewing it in hindsight.

Freaks and Geeks (1999–2000)

Before Seth Rogen, Jason Segel, James Franco, and Linda Cardellini were starring in Hollywood blockbusters, they were coming of age on the set of *Freaks and Geeks*. In addition to its stellar cast, the show—which tells the story of siblings Lindsay (Cardellini) and Sam Weir (John Francis Daley) trying to navigate high school from two different social standings—may be best known for its early cancellation: It ran for a single eighteen-episode season before it was pulled off the air in 2000.

It may not have received all the love it deserved during its run, but *Freaks and Geeks* has grown into a cult classic. It beat *Stranger Things* to the eighties nostalgia trend by almost two decades and is one of the most painfully accurate portrayals of high school life ever seen on the small screen (or big screen, for that matter). The career trajectories of the actors and filmmakers behind the show have also helped its legacy. Series creator Paul Feig and executive producer Judd Apatow both went on to become comedy heavyweights in spite of *Freak and Geeks*'s untimely end—or, perhaps, because of it. During a Q&A in 2008, Apatow asserted that

CLASS STRUGGLES

"Everything I've done, in a way, is revenge for the people who canceled *Freaks and Geeks*."

To make the series as painfully awkward and accurate as possible, and to jump-start the writing process, Feig had writers fill out questionnaires about their own high school experiences. Questions included: "What was the best thing that happened to you in high school? What's the most humiliating thing that happened to you in high school? What's the first sexual thing you ever did?" The answers were used to create the show's storylines. One exception to this autobiographical approach was made for episode seventeen, "The Little Things," in which Ken (Seth Rogen) is dating someone with ambiguous genitalia. (And in case you're wondering: Yes, Feig really did buy—and wear—a Parisian night suit to school.)

REPLAY

Future star of *The Big Bang Theory* and *The Flight Attendant* Kaley Cuoco auditioned for the role of *Freaks and Geeks*'s Cindy Sanders, the cheerleader Sam Weir (John Francis Daley) spends much of the series crushing on . . . until he actually dates her and learns that she doesn't think *The Jerk* is funny.

Riverdale (2017–present)
Based on the classic Archie Comics, *Riverdale* takes a darker, *Twin Peaks*-esque twist on characters Archie Andrews, Veronica Lodge, Betty Cooper, and Jughead Jones. For one, this show has a *whole lot* of murder, which is part of what initially draws fans into the series. But even after one mystery is solved— or at least seems to be— *Riverdale* continues to deliver the kind of addicting storylines that keeps fans eagerly anticipating when the next season will drop.

While it might be obvious to some die-hard fans, many viewers may not realize the significance of every episode title of *Riverdale*.

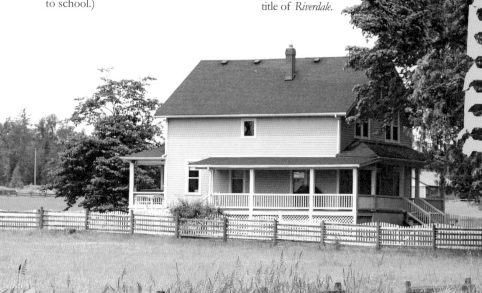

All the episodes are the names of, or a variation of the names of, old movies. These titles serve a purpose, as they hint at the storylines to come, giving serious cineastes a leg up when it comes to predicting what might happen in an episode titled "Body Double," "The Lost Weekend," "The Town That Dreaded Sundown," "Dog Day Afternoon," or "Fire Walk with Me" (there's that *Twin Peaks* influence).

In 2017, *Archie Comics*'s chief creative officer Roberto Aguirre-Sacasa, who developed the series, explained to *Teen Vogue* how much the episode titles reveal: "We usually work on the episode, and then, as we're going to the end of the breaking of the story, we're like, 'What's the title of this episode?' And then we have a list of provocative titles. Often the stories guide us."

Euphoria (2019–present)

Based on the Israeli miniseries of the same name, *Euphoria* was created by Sam Levinson to explore the lives of a diverse group of teenagers through their experiences with sex, drugs, friendships, love, identity, and trauma. Zendaya won a Primetime Emmy Award for Best Actress for her performance in season one (making her the youngest recipient in history for that category) as recovering drug addict Rue Bennett. But the generally enthusiastic praise for the show's unvarnished honesty in portraying its characters' lives was offset by criticisms of its decision to depict their sexuality in an equally fearless and often graphic way.

Levinson drew on his own teenaged experiences for Rue's storyline and frequently pulled stories from the lives of his young actors for inspiration in order to make the show and its storytelling more authentic.

MATCH THE TEACHER TO THE TV SHOW:

_____ I. George Feeny

_____ 2. Ms. Grundy

_____ 3. Mr. Kowchevski

_____ 4. Annalise Keating

_____ 5. Dr. Jack Griffin

_____ 6. Chuck Noblet

_____ 7. Valerie Frizzle

A. *Freaks and Geeks*

B. *Strangers with Candy*

C. *Boy Meets World*

D. *The Magic School Bus*

E. *Riverdale*

F. *How to Get Away with Murder*

G. *A.P. Bio*

What was your favorite show when you were in high school?

DOES IT STILL HOLD UP?

PEP TALKS

They may stand on the sidelines, but the best fictional coaches—
from cheerleading to football—are more than just side characters.
Here are a few of TV's most memorable team leaders.

Friday Night Lights (2006–2011)

Friday Night Lights executive producer Peter Berg wasn't keen on auditioning Kyle Chandler for the role of Coach Eric Taylor. At the time, Chandler was best known for playing a schoolboyish stockbroker on CBS's *Early Edition*, which was not the temperament Berg was looking for in Coach Taylor. But when Chandler showed up to their first meeting on a motorcycle, hot off a friend's birthday bash and looking scruffy, sleep-deprived, and extremely hungover, Berg changed his mind. "[He] goes, 'Whatever you did last night, I want you to keep doing it,'" Chandler said during a PaleyFest panel. "So I went home and said, 'Listen, honey . . . I have to smoke a lot of cigars, drink a lot of wine, and watch a lot of football.'"

Ted Lasso (2020–present)

After leading the Wichita State Shockers to a Division II college football championship, Ted Lasso (Jason Sudeikis) gets recruited to coach the *other* kind of football across the pond in this Golden Globe–winning Apple TV+ series. Though he's a fish out of water as a Premier League soccer club manager, Lasso proves his mettle as a top-notch sports mind and a genuinely great guy who cares about his team. Not bad for a character that was originally created to be a commercial mascot for NBC Sports when the network was promoting its airing of the English Premier League.

Glee (2010–2015)

Glee was far from a sports drama, but it had no shortage of coaches, including cutthroat cheerleading coach Sue Sylvester (Jane Lynch) and football coach Shannon Beiste (pronounced *Beast*), played by Dot-Marie Jones with a kind of raw intensity that would make Dick Butkus blush. But Coach Beiste is far from a one-note caricature. In *Glee*'s final season, the character is given real depth when Beiste comes out as transgender and announces his plans to transition— a rarity on network television.

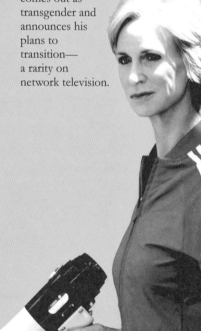

FILL IN THE BLANKS of these inspirational coaching quotes:

1. " _____ **does not exist in this dojo!"**

—JOHNNY LAWRENCE, *Cobra Kai*

2. **"I can't stand the sight of kids getting emotional, unless it's from _____ ."**

—SUE SYLVESTER, *Glee*

3. **"I believe in hope. I believe in _____ ."**

—TED LASSO, *Ted Lasso*

4. **"Clear eyes, _____ _____ , can't lose."**

—COACH TAYLOR, *Friday Night Lights*

5. **"I am the captain of the USS *Kick Ass*, not the USS _____ ."**

—COACH BEISTE, *Glee*

REPLAY

In 1996, legendary NFL player–turned–head coach Jim Harbaugh—who in 2013 became the first head coach to face off against his own brother, and fellow head coach, in a Super Bowl—appeared on an episode of *Saved by the Bell: The New Class*, playing himself . . . and the cousin of Dustin Diamond's Screech Powers.

SPOILED ROTTEN

Whether they spend their study breaks surfing or sitting on the steps of The Met, TV's rich kids deal with the same high-class problems.

The O.C. (2003–2007)

Josh Schwartz—who had never run a TV show before—was only twenty-six years old when he brought the idea of a nighttime teen soap to Fox, making him the youngest showrunner in the history of network television. Fox picked up the pilot to *The O.C.* and ordered an unprecedented twenty-seven episodes for the first season (the final season had just sixteen).

The O.C. premiered on August 5, 2003, early enough in the season that a lot of competing shows were still in reruns. It followed the lives of a group of affluent teens (and their parents) living in Newport Beach, California. But unlike predecessors like *Beverly Hills, 90210*, *The O.C.* focused more on character than plot and featured characters who were outsiders, such as Ryan Atwood (Ben McKenzie). The show was also self-aware in its humor.

Schwartz told *The New York Times* that he was a fan of canceled-too-soon shows like *Freaks and Geeks*, *Undeclared*, and *My So-Called Life*. "You can't tell a network that's what you want to make because they'll just say, 'Those shows lasted 15 episodes and they're off the air and we don't want them.' But if instead you go to Fox and say, 'This is your new *90210*'—that's something they can get excited about."

Schwartz and fellow executive producer Stephanie Savage pitched Fox the concept of a juvenile delinquent from Chino (Atwood) infiltrating

---

▶ REPLAY

If some of the more prominent locations on *Pretty Little Liars* look familiar, that's because the series was shot on the same set as *Gilmore Girls*. Emily Fields's (Shay Mitchell) front porch, for example, is also the Gilmores' front porch. And what *Pretty Little Liars* fans know as the Apple Rose Grille was Luke's Diner on *Gilmore Girls*. Look closely and you'll also see Stars Hollow's iconic gazebo pop up.

---

the glamorous world of Orange County's gated communities. "And really what we hoped we had were these characters that were a little bit funnier and more soulful and different and specific than the kinds you usually see in that genre," Schwartz said. "They would be the soldiers inside our Trojan horse."

Gossip Girl (2007-2012)

On September 19, 2007, just a few months after *The O.C.* squeezed the last bit of life out of its nighttime teen soap domination, Schwartz teamed with Stephanie Savage to swap the beachy vibes of California for the front steps of The Met with *Gossip Girl*. The series quickly became appointment television for America's teenagers—and a guilty pleasure for millions of non-teenagers.

Like a millennial version of *Beverly Hills, 90210*, the show—which was adapted from Cecily von Ziegesar's book series of the same name—follows the lives of a group of friends (and sometimes enemies) headed up by BFFs Serena van der Woodsen (Blake Lively) and Blair Waldorf (Leighton Meester) as they navigate the elite world of prep schools and just being plain fabulous on Manhattan's Upper East Side. They even learn to embrace the magical world of Brooklyn and its inhabitants—namely, the Humphrey family: Dan (Penn Badgley), Jenny (Taylor Momsen), and Rufus (Matthew Settle)—while the eponymous and ever-watchful blogger Gossip Girl tracks their every move and misstep.

Pretty Little Liars (2010-2017)

The dark, suspenseful tone of *Pretty Little Liars* makes it unique in the world of teen girl media. Loosely based on Sara Shepard's YA book series, it follows a clique of five friends—Spencer Hastings (Troian Bellisario), Alison DiLaurentis (Sasha Pieterse), Aria Montgomery (Lucy Hale), Hanna Marin (Ashley Benson), and Emily Fields (Shay Mitchell)—who drift apart when their leader Alison goes missing. A year after the disappearance, the girls reconnect when they start receiving threatening messages simply signed "A."

Part teen soap opera, part thriller, the series quickly attracted a devoted fan base of viewers eager to untangle the mystery. Fans who are hungry for more from the *Pretty Little* universe can watch *Ravenswood* and *Pretty Little Liars: The Perfectionist*. A third spin-off series titled *Pretty Little Liars: Original Sin* is set to premiere on HBO Max.

If you could raid one television character's closet, whose would you choose? _____

WHY? _____

_____

_____

MATCH THE THEME SONG WITH THE TEEN DRAMA:

_____ 1. "I Don't Want to Wait"   A. *One Tree Hill*

_____ 2. "Secret"   B. *Dawson's Creek*

_____ 3. "California"   C. *The O.C.*

_____ 4. "Here with Me"   D. *Pretty Little Liars*

_____ 5. "I Don't Want to Be"   E. *Roswell*

SHOW: _____

HOLE: _____

_____
_____
_____
_____

SHOW: _____

HOLE: _____

_____
_____
_____
_____
_____
_____

TV PLOT
HOLES
THAT ALWAYS
BUGGED ME

SHOW: _____

HOLE: _____

_____
_____
_____
_____
_____
_____
_____

SHOW: _____

HOLE: _____

_____
_____
_____
_____
_____

SHOW: _____

HOLE: _____

_____
_____
_____
_____
_____
_____

SHOW: _____

HOLE: _____

_____
_____
_____
_____

SHOWS THAT SUCK

Vampires have made a comeback in recent years,
and these are the ones you'll most want to take a bite out of.

Buffy the Vampire Slayer (1997–2003)
A lot of people can say that high school was hell, but for Buffy Summers (Sarah Michelle Gellar) and her peers, the horrors of young adulthood were truly demonic. Whether dealing with the undead consequences of sleeping with your first love or being literally silenced in an episode about the difficulty of communicating one's true self, *Buffy*'s simple stroke of genius was using monster movie genre conventions in service of deeply human stories.

Buffy, which began life as a little-seen 1992 movie starring Kristy Swanson and Luke Perry, celebrated the power and pain of relying on other people. The show, however, made it clear that even for a superhero protagonist living atop a portal to infernal dimensions, "the hardest thing in this world is to live in it."

In the *Buffy* movie, the vampires looked like regular people, only with sharper teeth and paler skin. But for the TV show, Whedon wanted to increase the sense of paranoia by making the vampires resemble normal people until it was time to feed—at which point, they transformed into monsters. It was both a stylistic choice and a

logical one. "I didn't think I really wanted to put a show on the air about a high school girl who was stabbing normal-looking people in the heart," Whedon said. "I thought somehow that might send the wrong message, but when they are clearly monsters, it takes it to a level of fantasy that is safer."

True Blood (2008–2014)
Set in fictional Bon Temps, Louisiana, Oscar winner Alan Ball's *True Blood* deals with vampires trying to acclimate to living among humans, sometimes with violent results. The Japanese invent a synthetic blood beverage called Tru Blood, which is meant to satiate vampires so they won't seek out real blood—but it doesn't work out so well.

Ball, creator of *Six Feet Under*, based the show on Charlaine Harris's *Sookie Stackhouse* book series. Sookie (Anna Paquin), part fairy and part telepathic human, falls in love with Bill (Stephen Moyer), a 173-year-old vampire (in 2010, Moyer and Paquin married in real life). Sookie is also drawn to Eric (Emmy winner Alexander Skarsgård) and shape-shifting werewolf Alcide (Joe Manganiello).

The idea for the series began with a trip to the dentist. Ball had to get a root canal and showed up thirty minutes early to his appointment. With time to kill, he visited a Barnes & Noble across the street and saw Charlaine Harris's book *Dead until Dark*, the first in a series of thirteen novels. "The tagline is, 'Maybe having a vampire for a boyfriend isn't such a bright idea,' which made me laugh," Ball told Emmy TV Legends. Ball, who grew up in Georgia, was also intrigued by the book's Southern feel. "It was this great mix of drama and comedy and horror and sex and violence and social commentary. She walked this line that was so incredibly entertaining that I couldn't put the book down." At the time, the book was under option to be made into a film, but when the option expired, Ball jumped at the chance to grab the rights for himself. He filmed a pilot and two more episodes, and HBO greenlit the series. *True Blood* blended sex, violence, and humor in a way no HBO show had done before—which led to it becoming the network's highest-rated show since *The Sopranos* (at least until *Game of Thrones* came along in 2011 and surpassed both shows).

In late 2020, HBO announced that it

REPLAY

If you want to see what would happen if the most famous vampires in pop culture got together, "The Trial," a season one episode of *What We Do in the Shadows,* features an all-star lineup of actors who have previously played iconic vampires on TV and in movies. Tilda Swinton (*Only Lovers Left Alive*), Evan Rachel Wood (*True Blood*), Danny Trejo (*From Dusk till Dawn*), and Paul Reubens (*Buffy the Vampire Slayer*) are among the episode's guest stars—while Wesley Snipes chimes in via Skype, playing his Daywalker character from the *Blade* movies.

was working on a reboot of *True Blood* and that Ball would serve as executive producer. The network also made it clear that it would be taking its time to get it right, leading to an extended development process with virtually no further details being leaked.

What We Do in the Shadows (2019–present)

If you're looking for laughs in your next binge-watch, you'd be hard-pressed to find something better than FX's *What We Do in the Shadows*, a mockumentary horror-comedy TV series about four vampires living a mostly mundane life in Staten Island. The series, which was born from the brains of *Flight of the Conchords*'s Jemaine Clement and Oscar winner Taika Waititi, delivers an absurdist version of the worries vampires might face in their modern day-to-day (non)lives.

A lot of people know that FX's *What We Do in the Shadows* is a small-screen spin-off of Waititi and Clement's 2014 movie of the same name. What fewer people realize is that *that* movie was an expansion of their 2005 short film, *What We Do in the Shadows: Interviews with Some Vampires*, which starred the same core cast as the feature. Nor do they realize that the FX series isn't the movie's first small-screen spin-off: *Wellington Paranormal*, a series about a New Zealand police department dealing with otherworldly events of all stripes, was the first TV show to air as part of the *What We Do in the Shadows* universe. It premiered on New Zealand's TVNZ 2 in July 2018 and finally came to the United States in 2021 via The CW and HBO Max.

If I had to spend the rest of eternity stuck in a house with three other TV vampires, I'd choose:

1 _____

WHY: _____

_____

_____

2 _____

WHY: _____

_____

_____

3 _____

WHY: _____

_____

_____

MATCH THE POP CULTURE VAMPIRE TO THE APPROPRIATE TV SHOW:

____ 1. Russell Edgington

____ 2. Katherine Pierce

____ 3. Colin Robinson

____ 4. Countess Elizabeth

____ 5. Benny Lafitte

____ 6. Thomas Eichorst

____ 7. Proinsias Cassidy

____ 8. John Mitchell

A. *American Horror Story: Hotel*

B. *What We Do in the Shadows*

C. *Preacher*

D. *The Vampire Diaries*

E. *True Blood*

F. *Supernatural*

G. *Being Human*

H. *The Strain*

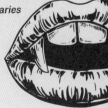

THE GOOD, THE BAD & THE UNDEAD

Death is no laughing matter . . . unless you're watching *The Good Place*.

The Good Place (2016–2020)

In 2016, NBC started airing the comedy *The Good Place*, an unusual sitcom about dead people who have been sent to the heaven-like afterlife called The Good Place. Kristen Bell stars as Eleanor, who should be in The Bad Place (Hell) but mistakenly gets sent to the former. Michael (Ted Danson) is the architect of The Good Place, whose residents include the name-dropping Tahani (Jameela Jamil), the at-first silent monk Jianyu, who's later revealed to be a dimwitted DJ named Jason (Manny Jacinto), the indecisive ethics professor Chidi (William Jackson Harper), and the Siri-esque Janet (D'Arcy Carden).

But nothing is ever what it seems to be on *The Good Place* (or in The Good Place), as viewers quickly learned in the show's first season. While, on the surface, the show had seemed like just another quirky comedy, showrunner Michael Schur—who co-created *Parks and Recreation*—wanted to make a sitcom with a message. And viewers went along for the ride, finding all sorts of philosophical lessons to be learned over the course of its four seasons. But as Schur told *The Hollywood Reporter* in 2016, the show wasn't about one religion's interpretation of the afterlife; it was about ethics. "It is very flatly stated that this is not any one religion," he said. "Spiritual and ethical is how I thought of it."

THE GOOD PLACE STAR TED DANSON HAS STARRED IN SEVERAL TV SERIES, AND EARNED MORE THAN 15 EMMY NOMINATIONS AS A RESULT. WHICH OF THE FOLLOWING DID *NOT* EARN HIM AN EMMY NOD?

_____ 1. *The Good Place*

_____ 2. *Cheers*

_____ 3. *Fargo*

_____ 4. *Something About Amelia*

_____ 5. *Damages*

Six Feet Under
(2001-2005)

As the title implies, death is everywhere in *Six Feet Under*. Alan Ball's critically-acclaimed HBO series begins with the death of Fisher family patriarch Nathaniel (Richard Jenkins), who runs the Fisher & Sons funeral home out of the family's California home with youngest son David (future *Dexter* star Michael C. Hall, in his first starring television role), who is struggling with his sexual orientation. When Nathaniel passes the family business on to David and his older brother, Nate (Peter Krause), Nate is forced to move back to California and get to know his family again—including mother Ruth (Frances Conroy) and teenage sister Claire (Lauren Ambrose).

Though it's a show about death—each episode kicks off with a death sequence, some of which can be truly bizarre and even disturbing—*Six Feet Under* is really about family and making the most of every moment of our lives. The series connected with viewers in a way few shows have ever managed, so much so that some people seemed to have trouble differentiating between TV magic and the real world. Jenkins once shared a story about how he attended a funeral while the show was still on the air and a fellow mourner tapped him on the shoulder to ask, "Are they filming this?"

Pushing Daisies
(2007-2009)

Television producer Bryan Fuller created something special with *Pushing Daisies*. The self-described "forensic fairy tale" was too fantastical for TV viewers, but too kooky and strange for moviegoers. It's the story of a pie maker named Ned (Lee Pace), proprietor of The Pie Hole pastry shop, but pie making is just one of his talents. He can also revive the dead with a single touch. Unfortunately, a second touch kills them again, permanently. His gift proves especially problematic when he revives Charlotte "Chuck" Charles (Anna Friel), his childhood sweetheart, after she is mysteriously murdered.

Initial enthusiasm for the series led to a full season order in October 2007, just weeks before a writer's strike was declared. This meant that the series had to halt production with only nine of its twenty-two ordered episodes completed. Fuller rewrote episode nine to serve as a season finale, leaving lots of loose ends to entice viewers back. It worked: *Pushing Daisies* got a second season, but its ratings weren't enough to keep this series alive. For years, fans have been begging for a reboot. In 2015, *Esquire* ran a TV Reboot Tournament in which readers voted for the shows they wanted to see come back, and *Pushing Daisies* beat out *Firefly* for the most missed series.

What are some of your favorite series finales?

WHY?

WHY?

WHY?

Two Degrees of...
Ted Danson

Fill in the title of the TV show or movie that connects these actors to *The Good Place* star Ted Danson.

PETER DINKLAGE
was in

_____
TV SHOW OR MOVIE NAME
(2018) with Idris Elba, who was in

_____
TV SHOW OR MOVIE NAME
(2008) with Ted Danson.

BETTY WHITE
was in

_____
TV SHOW OR MOVIE NAME
(2003) with Queen Latifah, who was in

_____
TV SHOW OR MOVIE NAME
(2002) with Ted Danson.

SOFIA VERGARA
was in

_____
TV SHOW OR MOVIE NAME
(2015) with Hope Davis, who was in

_____
TV SHOW OR MOVIE NAME
(1999) with Ted Danson.

MICHAEL B. JORDAN
was in

TV SHOW OR MOVIE NAME
(2015) with Tim Blake Nelson, who was in

TV SHOW OR MOVIE NAME
(2012) with Ted Danson.

NEIL PATRICK HARRIS
was in

TV SHOW OR MOVIE NAME
(2014) with Ryan Reynolds, who was in

TV SHOW OR MOVIE NAME
(2012) with Ted Danson.

JANE LYNCH
was in

TV SHOW OR MOVIE NAME
(1993) with Joe Pantoliano, who was in

TV SHOW OR MOVIE NAME
(2005) with Ted Danson.

HIDDEN GEMS

Viewers always want more of a good thing, but not all shows are able or willing to give it to them. These series were fun while they lasted—which wasn't long.

Detectorists (2014–2017)

In a sea of too-hip sarcasm and dark shows about dark men turning dark, this humble comedy is a comforting island of gentle gags and metal detectorist rivalries in an otherwise quiet and quaint English village. Andy (Mackenzie Crook, a.k.a. *The Office*'s Gareth Keenan) and Lance (Toby Jones) are two amateur treasure hunters who are obsessed with discovering interesting things underground and occasionally looking up to see if their personal lives are falling apart. Their world blossoms after an attractive college student named Sophie (Aimee-Ffion Edwards) joins their local Danebury Metal Detecting Club. It is the Holy Grail of sweet, sympathetic British comedies.

Game of Thrones fans will delight at seeing the late Diana Rigg having the time of her life as the mother of Andy's girlfriend, Becky, who is played by Rigg's real-life daughter, Rachael Stirling. Crook also wrote and directed all nineteen episodes of the show, winning two BAFTAs for his work.

REPLAY

Johnny Flynn, the British actor best known for his starring turn in the Netflix series *Lovesick*, playing David Bowie in the 2020 biopic *Stardust*, and playing George Knightley to Anya Taylor-Joy's Emma Woodhouse in *Emma* (2020), also wrote the opening theme for *Detectorists* and served as the series' composer. He even made a brief cameo in its third season. Johnny is the half-brother of fellow actor Jerome Flynn, who played the lovable sellsword Bronn in *Game of Thrones*.

One Mississippi (2015–2017)

Comedian Tig Notaro mined parts of her own life—including her well-documented battle with breast cancer and subsequent double mastectomy—to co-create the deeply funny dysfunctional family dramedy *One Mississippi* with Diablo Cody, the Oscar-winning screenwriter of *Juno*. In the partly autobiographical series, Notaro returns to her hometown near New Orleans in the wake of her mother's unexpected death and ends up staying there while she continues her own recovery from breast cancer.

Even when the material isn't exactly ripe for laughs, Notaro's natural humor shines through. In the final episodes, Notaro and Cody seemed to take a sort of creative revenge on Louis C. K., who had an executive producer credit on the short-lived series, despite Notaro's very public protestations.

Baskets (2016–2019)

This FX comedy stars Zach Galifianakis as twin brothers—failed theatrical clown Chip Baskets and quirky dad Dale Baskets—and Louie Anderson as their mom. After attempting to set the clowning world on fire in Paris, Chip returns home to California a broken man. The only option available to his very particular set of skills is taking a gig as a rodeo clown in Bakersfield, where he epitomizes the deadpan magic that Galifianakis has spent decades honing. It's a family comedy, but the laughs are more funny-strange than funny-ha-ha (although with his completely stoic delivery about a VW Beetle trunk being able to hold fifty clowns, Galifianakis may have pioneered something closer to funny-sad).

With a minuscule audience of fewer than 350,000 viewers, it's a miracle that we got four seasons of this smart, stealthily sweet show. In any other era, this would have been canceled before it finished its first. It's clear that it's not for everyone, but it might just be for you.

Russian Doll (2019–present)

Nadia (Natasha Lyonne) is having a bad night because she keeps dying. Whether it's slamming into a speeding cab or falling down a tricky flight of stairs, she's stuck in one of those aggravating time loop situations where her death brings her right back to the bathroom at her unwanted birthday party.

When she meets Alan (Charlie Barnett) and realizes he's going through the same thing, they team up to figure out what's going on and how to break the cycle. As with Bill Murray's character in *Groundhog Day* resetting to Sonny and Cher's "I Got You Babe," Nadia's reset song is "Gotta Get Up" by Harry Nilsson. The producers considered using Lou Reed's "Crazy Feeling," Lil' Kim's "Not Tonight," and The Stooges' "No Fun," in case you want to make a doom-loop playlist. *Russian Doll* is an amazing show that approaches the time loop concept with fresh ideas and bold characters, creating a perfect season of television that's all set to swing for the fences in season two.

Which show would you love to see just *one* more season of?

_____

WHY?

_____

_____

_____

OF THE BEST TV SERIES FINALES OF ALL TIME

1 Breaking Bad // "Felina"
Few series finales have ever faced such high expectations and managed to rise to meet them so powerfully as *Breaking Bad* did in 2013. "Felina" has everything you could ever want from a *Breaking Bad* send-off: Walt's final conversation with Skyler, an incredible revenge shoot-out, one main character's cry of freedom, and another's smile of victory. Some series finales deliver what you want; others deliver what you need. "Felina" somehow managed to do both.

2 Six Feet Under // "Everyone's Waiting"
The final minutes of "Everyone's Waiting" are among the most famous in the history of television, and even if the rest of the episode had been a disappointment, it would still rank among the greatest farewells in the medium. As it is, *Six Feet Under*'s final hour with the Fisher family was a gripping, heartfelt, and bitterly funny gem, all building to that last montage which, as Sia's "Breathe Me" plays, reminded us that death takes many forms beyond mere tragedy.

What makes a great TV series finale? Typically, it's one that ties up loose ends without being annoyingly completist or overly sentimental. Here are a handful of shows that have done it well.

3 The Americans // "Start"
The Americans quietly became one of the best shows on TV before finally winning a bunch of awards for its final season, and with good reason. The final adventures of Philip and Elizabeth Jennings, as they contemplate a return to Russia and an end